VIGNETTI
SMALL-TO

LiFE LESSONS FROM A LATE BLOOMER

JACKiE EWiNG

To Jennifer,
Enjoy the
ride &
Carpe Diem!
J. Ewing

This book is a work in the genre of creative non-fiction. Some individuals' names and identifying characteristics have been changed to maintain their anonymity. I have tried to recreate events, locales, and conversations from my memories of them. But I'm old. And, unlike wine, my memory doesn't seem to improve with age. Any mistakes are my own.

Dedicated to my children.

CONTENTS

Laughter sets the spirit free through even the most tragic circumstances. It helps us shake our heads clear, get our feet back under us and restores our sense of balance. Humor is integral to our peace of mind and our ability to go beyond survival.

— CAPTAIN GERALD COFFEE, POW,
Vietnam War, seven years

PREFACE

DECEMBER 1991

I'm a fashionista at heart. My ability to rock the "yoga pants and sweatshirt" look sparks envy even in Parisians themselves. However, I haven't always had my finger so firmly planted on the pulse of haute couture.

As a young kindergarten teacher, the halls of an American international school in Kuwait City were my runways and I strutted them in dresses and heels. Although the job description included daily floor sitting, I felt invincible in my attire.

As I became more comfortable in my teaching role, my style confidence grew. Pastel blouses dodged crayoned, food-eating, nose-picking fingers with ease, returning home each evening in pristine condition.

I reached my fashion pinnacle on The Day of the Cream-Coloured Dress. Which happened to coincide with art class. And paint. Bright green paint intended for giant cardboard Christmas trees. These were not play-it-safe, elementary school-aged appropriate, diffident, paint pucks. Oh no. The paint on The Day of the Cream-Coloured Dress arrived in vast, smirking vats.

My hubris knew no bounds.

Until, while dodging an errant scamp on a mission with one of the vats, I tripped.

Thick green paint splashed everywhere—blanketing my dress, face, and hair.

Staggering blindly across the hall to the cavernous kindergarten bathroom, I unwittingly became acquainted with a floor that had just been washed. Lying prone on the damp floor, green paint dripped down my hair into my eyes, 'Kill me now' raced through my mind. Maybe it was a sign to quit my job and drive a Diet Coke truck for a living. Spread-eagle, I succumbed to the moment in rueful resignation: "This is Your Life, Jacqueline Kate Ewing."

With uncanny timing, a stall door opened. Through a hazy film of green, I looked up to find my erstwhile scamp standing directly over me, pants and underwear around his ankles, hands on his butt crying,

"Miss Jackie, it's stuck, it's stuck. Help me get it out!"

Over the course of my life, I have encountered many green-paint moments, some funny, some not. Along the way I've managed to pick up a few life lessons. A slippery bathroom floor, even if only a metaphorical one, can be an astute teacher indeed.

So ... here's to green paint!

CHAPTER ONE

TO THINE OWN SELF BE TRUE

Had I realized as a teenager that by the ripe old age of fifty-five I would still be figuring out who I was, I might have deduced then that I was indeed a late bloomer. However, I realize now that figuring out who we are is a lifelong process for navel-gazers such as myself. Whether you fall in the "That's called narcissism" camp or "The unexamined life is not worth living" camp informs your viewpoint.

I don't like jigsaw puzzles; my spatial awareness quotient is low. I do like the finished product, though. Seeing all the individual pieces snap together to form a beautiful whole is satisfying. Even in myself. Maybe even especially in my navel-gazing self.

My physical and character traits all fit together to create a unique vision that's worthy of being glued down onto a canvas one day. I'm not complete yet—there are a few segments still left to be snapped more firmly into place. Hiding. Slyly nestled among carpet fibres. Under a napkin. Patiently waiting to be discovered and accepted. Sometimes I look at a piece in dismay, but with a change in perspective I grow to see both the beauty and the humour in the funky shapes that make me—well, me.

* * *

For twenty-eight blissful years, I remained happily unaware of my freakishly small head. Vacationing in Cyprus with my boyfriend, I had my ignorance shattered at the end of the idyllic holiday. We had flown into Larnaca, travelled around the island for a week, and then returned to the city for our flight out. As luck would have it, we ended up with the same taxi driver both times. I thought this was a cool coincidence and piped up, "Hey, remember us? You drove us a week ago."

To which she replied, all thick-accented and stony-faced, "YOU. I remember YOU. YOU with the small head."

Me. Me with the small head.

This explained so much. Why I bought sunglasses from the kids' carousel at the mall. Why hats always slip down into my eyes. Why my mother kept telling me that my brains were probably "just all in the back of my head."

Tiny-meloned Jackie.

✳ ✳ ✳

Fast-forward to my early fifties. I had an upcoming "procedure" booked. (As Billy Crystal says in *City Slickers*, "In your fifties you have a minor surgery. You'll call it a procedure, but it's a surgery."). One side of my thyroid had three nodules on it that had been slowly but steadily growing and were starting to affect my heart. I was sent for a variety of tests, the final ones being a stress test and an echocardiogram.

I lay down on the table as a woman entered to perform the ultrasound. Within minutes she started muttering. I ignored her. Her muttering grew louder. I cordially asked if everything was okay.

"Oh, Honey, my goodness, this is quite a rib cage you have here."

I responded with a "thank-you." Pride coursed through me. I may have a lumpy throat, but damn—I sure had me one prodigious rib cage.

Then she started patting my arm and telling me that it was all right.

"It's okay, Hon. That's just how God made you. But my goodness, I have never seen one this large in all my life."

She continued to pat my arm and reference God's brilliant rib cage design two more times. My pride deflated.

Riddled with consternation, I pondered how I was to get home. There wasn't a tent-coat big enough to hide my unsightly body from the world. As I sidled out of the hospital, thoughts of Cher filled my head. Surely, I had read somewhere that she had had ribs removed. Maybe they could pull a few of mine while removing my nodules.

Not a surgery—just a procedure.

✳ ✳ ✳

I have been blessed and cursed with long, thin arms and long, thin legs. I remember reading *The Chrysalids* in high school and thinking that I would have been banished from the community and sent to the Fringes for my lack of average-sized limbs. An abomination. A deviant.

As a gangly child and equally gangly teen-ager, I despaired of my skinniness. I was forever trying to gain weight and even kept track with a calorie book: "Four pieces of toast laden with pea-nut butter and brown sugar—no weight gain." I laugh wryly at this now while I shake my fist in the air. "Curse you, middle-aged spread!"

As I settled into my looks, I began to appreciate my mutated limbs: short, short skirts, high, high heels, not a chafed thigh to be found—the benefits were piling up.

I was feeling pretty good about myself physically around the time I went for a dress-fitting in Kuwait. Two young tailors were measuring me. They kept murmuring, "Just like Barbie."

I demurred, "Oh stop, you're making me blush."

Suddenly, they started pushing up my breasts.

"Nipples at armpits, must be at armpits," the women kept repeating.

My girls were perky, but ... nipples at armpits? Who knew?

Now, deeply entrenched in the perimenopausal stage of life, I am just grateful that they're not at my belly button.

✷ ✷ ✷

As an inveterate reader, I always immerse myself in the stories I read. I relate to, nay, become the characters. I was alternately outspoken, adventur-ous Jo, kindhearted, gentle Beth in *Little Women*, or talk-a-mile-a-minute Anne in *Anne of Green Gables*. As I matured, I continued this habit, which was good for my husband while reading *50 Shades of Grey*, not so good while reading *The Husband Poisoner*.

I devoured the book *Wild* in a couple of days. Let me preface this by stating that I am not, in any way, shape, or form, athletic. I am routinely relegated to the sidelines during teacher-vs-student competitions.

After putting down *Wild* I was filled with enthusiasm. I was Cheryl Strayed and I would walk away from my earthly belongings and traverse the Pacific Crest Trail (PCT). I started researching my epic adventure: Bear spray! Backpacks! New boots! I would only pack items that were both fashionably cute and fully functional for weeks of introspective, life-altering hiking. I would commune with nature. I would rediscover my latent lust for adventure.

I would keep all my toenails. (Sorry, Cheryl.)

Brimming with ideas, I told my friends Sandra and Karla about the plan. Within minutes my proposal had changed to hike the Bruce Trail (Canada's longest footpath, spanning 900 kilometres). A few minutes later, it had morphed into a hike around the mall. Finally, one minute (and another drink) later, my adventure found its final form: a long weekend at a spa.

I haven't picked up *Wild* for several years now. Every time I think of it, I realize that I am in desperate need of a facial.

This "idea/plan/fail to execute" cycle is an unfortunate pattern in my life. Darned follow-through gets me every time. I salute my niece who does not struggle with this affliction and is, in actual fact, currently hiking the entire PCT. Her nails have stayed intact.

✳ ✳ ✳

Birth order personality types is a real thing. I state this with confidence, not solely based on my many years of teaching kids (and being able to pick out quickly and accurately who is an only, a first, a last, and a middle), but also from firsthand experience. I have an older sister and two younger brothers. Lisa is two years older than me, I'm two years older than Doug, and Doug is six years older than David. Lisa is a stereotypical firstborn: organized, achievement oriented, and take-charge.

Thank goodness for firstborns, because Lisa has saved us from ourselves more times than I can count. She has hosted a plethora of birthday gatherings, anniversary parties, and family reunions. The rest of us might not actually know anyone's birthday if not for her annual, clearly marked calendars. We have ridden her coattails many a time, especially on major milestone birthdays. Exquisitely decorated tables, thoughtful gifts, mouthwatering food and wine in a league of its own. She and my brother-in-law Richard made it all look so easy.

One year she passed the mantle. It was my mother's birthday—I don't remember which one, but clearly not a major milestone or no mantle would have been passed. Aided and abetted by my brother David, I wanted to show everyone that we too could pull off a laid-back celebration while maintaining a go-with-the-flow attitude. We confidently told Lisa and Doug that the celebration was in capable hands.

Mom's favourite meal at the time was fish and chips from a local restaurant, so David and I decided takeout was the perfect food choice. The day arrived. Tragedy struck early though, when we realized that we had failed to procure a cake. We called the local grocery stores and bakeries but to no avail. In hindsight, I'm not sure why we didn't just pick up a frozen cake from the supermarket, but I think we wanted it to at least *appear* homemade. Thankfully, Tim Horton's came to the rescue! David and I confidently sauntered in and leaned on the countertop. They had one cake left. One beautifully made chocolate cake with chocolate icing and red trim. Tragedy averted and we hadn't even broken a sweat. Watch and learn, firstborns.

There was just one small glitch—the icing read: "Happy Retirement Bob."

Sorry, Bob.

We picked up the fish and chips and brought it home. Into the oven it all went for a little warm-up.

David and I smugly congratulated ourselves for the successful undertaking. It was just about this time that an unpleasant odor began to assault our noses. We raced to the oven only to find we had put the food in the oven while it was still in Styrofoam containers. The smell was burning Styrofoam. Toxic, burning Styrofoam.

Goodbye, fish and chips. Hello, grilled cheese sandwiches with a side of ketchup.

Then we did what any self-respecting birthday revellers would do: we sang "Happy Retirement" to Bob.

My brother and I gave Mom a truly memorable birthday. That has to count for something, right?

Lisa hosted the next twenty years of birthdays.

✳ ✳ ✳

My wanderlust tendencies, which came to fruition as an adult, were evident as a young child.

I spent five years growing up in a small town where I had the good fortune to live kitty-corner to the McClement family. They were a large family with nine kids, ranging from six-year-old Kim to married Rosemary. Kim became my first buddy. I am amazed when I think back now to how unstructured our time was. There was a sprawling furniture factory half a block away, which became our de facto playground on weekends and evenings. We especially loved climbing through a broken window on the main floor—it was a good place to play jacks on rainy days. The railroad track right by our homes provided an amusement park venue. Putting our ears on the rails for vibrational hints that a train was imminent became a common pastime. Yelling "Train!" and jumping off into the grassy banks was more exciting than a trip to Disneyland. We would play kick the can and literally run all over town. Kids roamed the streets outside after school until supper and then would idle away the hours out-of-doors again until it got dark.

Kim had three older brothers and an expansive yard. At some point the boys built Kim a fort. It was a large, triangular-shaped building made of wood, with solid stairs leading into it, sheltered by a shingled roof. Yellow and blue floral curtains graced the glass-paned windows, and dishes and chairs were supplied to supplement the small table.

Bunk beds finished it off.

It was a thing of beauty. We watched its progress with bated breath and finally the big day arrived. Our majestic edifice was complete.

Arriving back home from school, I skipped upstairs and confidently started to pack. Calling out a breezy goodbye to my mom and dad, I explained that I would be back shortly to collect my pillow, sleeping bag and some food. When my poor, bewildered parents asked me where I was going, I calmly stated that I was moving out. I had my own house now, I had a fun roommate, and they could forward my mail.

They eventually stopped laughing and explained that in fact no, I could not actually live on my own. That I was legally tied to them in this feudal system and to unpack my things, brush my teeth, and get ready for bed, thank you very much.

Brimming with self-righteous indignation, I sulked, yelled, and cried but ended up—between shooting contemptuous, scathing looks at poor Mom and Dad—brushing my teeth and getting ready for bed.

My dreams of independence and adventure would have to be put on hold until my mid-twenties, when my thirst for travel and new experiences would take me to live and explore faraway countries all over the world.

A year later we moved, but I never forgot the McClements or the triangular-shaped haven. A veritable palace to six-year-olds.

Coolest fort ever.

✷ ✷ ✷

Kind and gentle are lovely adjectives that I have often heard used to describe me. Another that springs to mind is "stubborn." Good God, I can be stubborn. This trait is best displayed in The Great Sleeping Bag Battle of 1975.

We were all sitting around our pine-scented, scrubbed, rectangular kitchen table in Walkerton, Ontario, eating dinner. The six of us ate together each night and regularly participated in the setting of the table, cleaning of the dishes, and sweeping of the floor. I have no memory of the main course that evening but there is no doubt that the vegetable served was ... peas.

I hated peas. The texture, the taste, even the look of them.

I hated peas.

The meal wore on and eventually it came to my parents' attention that I was not eating my vegetables. One by one, my siblings finished their food and left the table. I had to finish my peas before I could get down.

I would not eat my peas.

Eventually, my dad abandoned us, and I was left with my mom, who sipped her tea until she too deserted me for her nightly viewing of *Wheel of Fortune*.

Time passed.

One by one, my siblings headed off to bed, but I remained resolute.

I would not eat my peas.

The empty table seemed infinite, and the kitchen echoed with silence. My parents regularly popped back in to see if I had broken, only to receive a scornful stare. Who would swerve first in this vegetable game of Chicken?

Finally, Doug came down with a sleeping bag for me. Doors were locked, front porch lights turned off, and the main floor was emptied. It was just me, my sleeping bag, and a pile of green peas.

Time passed. At long last, my parents came back downstairs, housecoats haphazardly thrown over pajamas, hair mussed, rubbing their hands over their eyes.

"Jac," they sighed, "you win. Throw them out and get to bed."

They never forced me to eat peas again.

I would like to tell you that my stubbornness has abated over the years, but in truth, I'm just more adept at disguising it.

Stubborn as a rock.

I still do not eat peas.

***

I've been golden blonde, Marilyn Monroe-esque white blonde, dark brown, and a redhead. In my experience, hair colour doesn't correlate with ditzy behaviour. My gullible nature is follicly colour-blind.

The first sign of my all-too-trusting nature reared its ugly head when I was around five. Lisa and I had two goldfish, identical in size and shape (aren't they all?) named Flopsie and Mopsie. I remember almost nothing about those damned fish, and yet their very existence cast a spotlight on my naïveté and gave my siblings teasing fodder for years to come.

One morning Lisa woke up and made her way over to the fish tank.

"Jackie, your fish died," she said matter-of-factly.

Sure enough, one lonely fish was swimming around the bowl while the other was bobbing belly up on the water's surface. I took one look and burst into tears. It was my first brush with death. I was inconsolable, but Lisa stoically patted my back and reassured me that all would be well.

It was years (and by that, I mean decades) later before I thought to ask how Lisa had known that it was *my* fish swimming in The Sea of the Great Beyond and not hers.

Suffice it to say that this was just the first of many times in my life when I too willingly took things at face value.

Maybe being gullible is simply having the quality of trusting people easily. That's kind of a nice quality to have—even if I do end up with some extra swampland in Florida along the way.

***

I recently completed a Myers-Briggs personality test and came out as a "Mediator INFP-T." The description was uncanny in its accuracy. What made me laugh out loud though, was the fun fact that this personality type was the most likely to do poorly under pressure.

It was 2001 and I was walking my Airedale terrier, Boomer, near the river in Ottawa. I love to walk, especially by myself. I find it a great time to relax, think, and get some fresh air.

It was a rainy, grey day in early June, and we had the paths mostly to ourselves. Seven-and-a-half months into my first pregnancy, I was not moving quickly—I was ambling. Meandering. Smelling the roses. Sashaying, even, along the bucolic trail.

My peace was shattered when Boomer started straining and barking. The leash slid out of my hands, and Man's Best Friend lunged into the woods towards the river. My repeated attempts to assert alpha control failed miserably, and I found myself following the sound of his progressively more frenetic barking.

I found him at the edge of the river, barking at a very large bear who was standing on his (I presumed it was male – aren't all predators male?) hind legs.

Did I try to make myself look large? Did I remain calm? Did I back away slowly? I did not. I froze, spun around, and ran like escaping prey, faintly calling Boomer as I ran.

If a camera had caught my attempted escape, the video would have gone viral in minutes: an exceedingly pregnant woman racing blindly through the underbrush, branches snapping at her face, hands waving frantically in the air. No longer ambling, nor meandering, and definitely not sashaying. I was trampling roses.

All that was flitting through my brain at lightning speed was dog aggravates bear, bear chases dog, dog runs faster than pregnant woman, pregnant woman gets devoured.

It's astonishing that I didn't go into premature labour on the spot.

It took a few minutes—what seemed like a lifetime—before I realized that surely, I would hear a large bear charging after me, even over the wild beating of my heart. Eventually, Boomer joined me, unharmed and swaggering (little-known fact:

dogs can indeed swagger), and we found our way back to civilization.

Twenty years later I still have a fear of bears. If you are ever hiking in the same woods as me, you will be able to pick me out as the woman religiously waving her bear bell and blowing her whistle every other step.

It's not a good look, but hey, I've never run into another bear. You do the math.

Calm and cool under pressure; that's me.

✳ ✳ ✳

"Every form of addiction is bad, no matter whether the narcotic be alcohol or morphine or idealism," said Carl Jung.

He didn't mention Diet Coke, but I'm sure it would have made the list. "Hi, my name is Jacqueline, and I am an addict."

I have been addicted to Diet Coke since I started university. Over the years, I have attempted to wean myself from this nectar of the gods but always end up falling off the wagon. This is the sign that hangs in my classroom (a gift from savvy students): "Never get between Ms. Ewing and her Diet Coke." It's not a secret.

The depth of my addiction was made obvious to me while on a camping trip in Algonquin Park with my first husband. Thoughts of days without cold Diet Coke (because of course it has to be cold) called for immediate action. No one wants to be trapped with a detoxing Jackie in the wild. I wish that we'd had a film crew videotaping us as we canoed along the lake, a string attached to the back of the canoe with six cans of Diet Coke dangling behind in the water. (Coca-Cola, contact me for more brilliant marketing ideas.)

This year I watched a Netflix show about Bill Gates, *Inside Bill's Brain*, and saw that he had an entire fridge stocked with Diet Coke. If one of the smartest men in the world drinks it to excess, surely, I can drink it guilt-free too.

There are worse addictions.

We can rationalize anything.

✳ ✳ ✳

Let me say that I would never be the witness the police turn to when trying to solve a crime. They would classify me as an unreliable narrator. I am flat-out unobservant. I may be highly attuned to every emotion in the room and able to tell you in seconds how people are feeling, but what they are wearing? No idea. This is in stark contrast to my childhood friend Sue, who can still recount which student sat in which row in public school and what they were wearing, down to the colour of the stripes on their socks.

My lack of attention to minutiae was evident during my first time at a bar. I was in grade 12, and my sister Lisa was attending university, majoring in business. Lisa had kindly lent me her ID that night, and I set off with a few friends to a bar in a nearby town. It took three visits to three different establishments before we met with success.

I airily explained to the male bartender with a languid wave of my hand, "I'm Lisa, and I'm in Biz."

I was smooth as silk and knew intuitively that it never crossed his mind we were underaged. Surely all drinkers tell their waiters their name and occupation unsolicited while ordering.

Riding the adrenaline high from this experience, I was oblivious to my surroundings. It took music starting and footsteps for me to zone in. Oh—there was a stage. Oh, wait, a girl was walking onto it. Oh my, she was barely dressed. Good God, she was dancing.

Turns out it wasn't only my first night in a bar but my first (and only) night in a strip club.

And no, her nipples were not level with her armpits either.

✴ ✴ ✴

I have concluded that I should say no to *The Bachelor* franchise when they come knocking on my door to pluck me from obscurity and catapult me into superstardom. Shocking, I know, since old married women rank highly on their list. As I watched with a mixture of voyeurism and revulsion alongside my daughter Molly and stepdaughter Madelynn, I realized I would be so intent on winning that I wouldn't be able to tell if I genuinely liked the guy.

You know that you have a competitiveness problem when you find yourself, beads of perspiration dripping down your forehead, barking out, "AGAIN. LET ME TRY IT AGAIN," while being tested for a position as a pants folder.

Yes, a pants folder.

You also know that you're an incredibly broke university student when you apply for a job as a pants folder. I needed rent money, and I needed it quickly, so, newspaper ad in hand, I went to the interview. I tried not to show my surprise when told that I would have to try out for the position, as many other people were interviewing.

Other people were interviewing? Game on, my friend, game on. Any form of competition and my frontal cortex (anterior cingulate cortex to be exact) goes into overdrive. A Terry Fox walk? Watch my feet. Mine will be an almost imperceptible-to-the-human-eye millimetre ahead of yours. Tell me that you don't think I can do something and then step aside. Reverse psychology works.

Several timed activities to determine my manual dexterity (my boyfriend could have attested to this) were prime real estate for my competitive nature to take up residence. Add this to the fact that my results were going to be compared to the five other applicants', and it was go time.

I nailed that pants-folding test.

Drenched in sweat I looked around with a "take that, suckers!" glare as I figuratively dropped a mic. It took a second for me to breathe again and realize that I had just won the opportunity to ... fold pants.

If only I could use my competitive superpower for good.

✶ ✶ ✶

I have been labelled rash by some. However good-intentioned, some over-the-top decisions made on the fly might require curtailing—or at the very least, allocated more than two seconds of forethought.

Teaching my grade one students was a joy. I loved finding innovative ways to bring out the best in each student. Observing a child who struggled with reading and writing and had already self-identified as "the dumb kid" at the age of six broke my heart. Music, art, physical fitness, interpersonal skills, affinity with nature ... multiple intelligence often got underestimated. When someone in my class overcame a fear, passed a milestone, or completed a challenging task, I was all in to celebrate. Sometimes, my whole class needed a shout-out: for walking quietly in the halls, staying on task for an extended period, helping each other—the opportunities were endless. I would pretend to faint in astonishment, but since the classroom floor was quite hard and cold, more often I chose to dance.

My bragging dance became a thing, and I would boogie my way around the room, freestyling in celebration. These hips cannot be contained.

Winter is long where I live. Some years, flakes arrive at the end of October and don't take their snowy leave until April. A procedural writing lesson involving creating s'mores and having a pretend campfire with a real sing-along, aided by novice guitar player Jackie, was something that added a little cheer to the cold, dark days.

One reticent little girl in my class really struggled with language. She worked with firm resolve on each step of the process, and at long last held her finished product out to me with shy pride and a cautious smile.

Well.

I saw a look on her face that I'd never seen. In R.J. Palacio's book *Wonder*, Auggie says, "Everyone deserves a standing ovation because we all over-cometh the world."

Auggie is the man.

This clearly called for The Bragging Dance. The other students started clapping for her, and I bopped around the room in pride. In my elation, I impetuously decided to take things to the next level. Jumping up on a low, blue, hexagonal table, I busted out my best actions for that young girl.

A few weeks later, parent-teacher interviews rolled around. I always enjoyed the chats and generally came out of them feeling like I knew my students better than I had going into them. One couple came in to discuss their son. They appeared rather humourless and provided little nonverbal feedback during the visit. A tough read. At the close of the interview, I asked if they had any other questions before leaving. They looked at each other and turned in unison to look at me. And then, deadpan, they asked, "Just one. Tell us—is it true that Ms. Ewing is a table dancer?" The corners of their mouths quirked up in grins.

Table-dancing Ms. Ewing retired the next day. Floor-dancing Ms. Ewing continues to occasionally dance a jig.

∗ ∗ ∗

If you had asked me as a child what I wanted to be when I grew up, I would unabashedly and unequivocally have said an actor. My flair for the dramatic made this a good fit. I excelled at public speaking (winning competitions in grades six, seven, and eight—I peaked young), memorized lines with ease, loved trying different accents, and lived for books and movies. There is even a tiny, minuscule chance that, when too much peace prevailed, I created drama for the sheer excitement of it. Sometimes this trait caused me trouble, but it also supplied plenty of amusement.

Our family childhood home was large, three-storied, and red-bricked with a wrap-around covered porch. Massive potted ferns were plentiful, scattered alongside chairs and a small, round table. Overgrown foliage surrounding the porch led friends to wonder if we were in the witness protection program. A rectangular hanging swing resided on one side of the porch. Most of my important life conversations with my parents happened on that swing. Maybe it's like talking while driving in a car—you're not looking directly at one another, and the motion is relaxing.

One afternoon in my second year of university, I was swinging with Mom when she took the opportunity to give me my first (and only) parental sex education talk. It went like this:

"They'll all try, Jac. Even the nice ones. Even *your father tried*. It's up to the girl to say no."

And there it was. My sex talk.

I gently explained that I had been dating Ted for many months now, was twenty years old and ... this girl hadn't said no. We swung in silence for a while. Finally, I asked her why she was shocked—after all, I'd slept over at Ted's many a night.

"I always had the faint hope that you were sleeping on the couch. Maybe ignorance really is bliss."

The next morning, I walked slowly down our long staircase, past my open-mouthed siblings and parents, staring stoically straight ahead while wearing a white top, white jeans, and a very large, very red, letter "A" affixed to my chest.

English major + flare for the dramatic = The Scarlet Daughter.

LIFE LESSON #1

EMBRACE YOURSELF AND DROP THE DEFENSIVENESS.

So, there you have it, a partial picture of what makes me unique, both physically and emotionally. The inimitable Jacqueline Kate Ewing. Perfectly imperfect. It has taken years to find and accept the puzzle pieces that make me who I am, the good, the bad, and the ugly. I don't profess to have mastered this process and indeed hope that I have many more years in which to grow as a person. The border is finished, but I still have some centre pieces yet to fill in.

One thing I know for sure—I value people who can laugh at themselves. It doesn't mean putting yourself down; just recognize that it's okay to look like an idiot sometimes.

Insight coupled with self-acceptance: that's the sweet-spot.

Getting angry and defensive when things go wrong does not make for a happy life. Things will go wrong. You will look like an idiot sometimes. You will have your own "Happy Retirement, Bob" moment, your own giant rib cage experience, and your own pregnant flight of fear.

When we get defensive, we shut down and go on the attack, like we need to defend our very core. It demonstrates that we can't regulate our emotions, that our skin is wafer-thin and our ability to deal with embarrassment is quite low. Defensiveness pushes people away. Accept yourself—including the times that you look like an idiot—and smile. It makes even the most embarrassing moments at least a little bit better.

Audrey Hepburn once said: "I love people who make me laugh. I honestly think it's the thing I like most, to laugh. It cures a multitude of ills. It's probably the most important thing in a person."

I concur, Audrey. But ... if no one else is making me laugh – I'm pretty darn good at cracking myself up, too.

I may be a navel-gazing narcissist, but at least I'm amusing myself along the way.

According to Socrates, "To know thyself is the beginning of wisdom." To this, Philosopher Jackie would add: To know and accept thyself without getting thy back up is the beginning of happiness.

CHAPTER TWO

OH, FOR THE LOVE OF LOVE

Maintaining healthy, happy relationships is the holy grail in life. Finding "your people," who accept, love, and like you *exactly the way you are* is worth its weight in gold.

As Robert Fulghum says, "We're all a little weird. And life is a little weird. And when we find someone whose weirdness is compatible with ours, we join up with them and fall into mutually satisfying weirdness—and call it love."

If I had a time machine, one of my main objectives would be to imbue younger Jackie with a stronger sense of self, and confidence that her weird people were out there.

I would also tell myself that I need to stop watching so many damned rom-coms. *Dirty Dancing*, *When Harry Met Sally*, *Sleepless in Seattle*, *You've Got Mail*, *Say Anything*, *Pretty Woman* ... the list goes on.

As Rosie O'Donnell's character tells Meg Ryan in *Sleepless*: "You don't want to be in love. You want to be in love *in a movie*."

Add the multitude of hours spent watching and rewatching romance to my affinity for relating to/ becoming fictional characters, and you end up with years of unrealistic expectations.

I should have been watching *He's Just Not That Into You*.

✱ ✱ ✱

I'm a bookworm, tea granny, lover of kittens, puppies, and have been known to listen to some Anne Murray on the sly. I am not a violent person. I reached my physical aggression pinnacle in grade one, and it's been downhill ever since.

There was a boy. Gary. Gary was the love of my six-year-old life. I wanted to play girls chase/ kiss the boys, with Gary as my prime target, every recess. I knew, deep in my soul, that Gary and I were destined to be together.

There was another boy. Danny. Danny liked

me. In fact, he liked me so much that he kissed me in the classroom.

And I ... I punched him in the stomach.

This was my one and only act of violence. I didn't punch him because he kissed me. Au contraire. I punched him because he kissed me *in front of Gary.* Gary would never be mine if he thought that Danny was my boyfriend. This act of rebellion was rewarded with punishment that had me standing in front of the class on one foot, both arms outstretched, holding two heavy books.

The shame.

I was probably only up there for a few minutes, but it felt like hours. Archaic though it seems looking back on it now, it was worth it. I took my punishment. As God was my witness, I would prove to Gary that I was his, and his alone.

The next day Gary told me that he liked Sylvia. Her desk was neater than mine.

And Danny? Why, Danny liked me just the way I was, messy desk and all. And for that I punched him.

It was the beginning of what would be years of choosing the wrong boys.

The writing was on the wall, people.

In my younger years, I was not a particularly good picker of men, often setting arbitrary parameters around my selection process that were unimportant in the grand scheme. Qualities like kindness, a sense of humour, and an easygoing nature didn't factor highly on my priority list. Muscles, excitement, and a brooding Heathcliff-style, manly-man-ness were much more enticing to my twenty-one-year-old self.

My university roommates and I decided to host a Halloween party at our house one year. I, a lover of punny costumes, decided to go as a Freudian Slip (inspired by Meg Ryan, *DOA*). I wore a slip (back when people still owned them) with the letters: F, R, E, U, D sewn across the front. This was my litmus test. I would save my Jackie-flirtatious best for the boys that "got" my costume. Anyone requiring an explanation would automatically be deemed unworthy.

Pickings were slim.

I grew tired of explaining myself as the night wore on and became more disheartened by the minute. For this I was freezing in my body-skimming slip?

I didn't realize then that it's easier to be clever than kind. How many nice, genuine, friendly guys did I miss out on that night? Maybe if I'd dressed up as a giant pumpkin instead I might have actually met someone interested in my sparkling personality. Where might I have ended up and with whom? Oh, the *Sliding Doors* variations were endless!

I was definitely a university snob. I'm ashamed to say this, but I didn't date anyone in college (In Canada, a university is more difficult to get into and is more academically rigorous than college, while in the US, for example, that distinction is not made.) or apprenticing for a trade. They weren't even on my radar. I didn't realize then that education level wasn't the only predictor of intelligence. It's funny now because my husband, Dave, is a college-educated man and one of the smartest people I know. His emotional intelligence is off the charts, and it's hard to find a person who doesn't love him. He has the unique ability to deliver the iron fist in the velvet glove at his high-stress job; has heated, passionate discussions about concepts way above my university-educated self; and still ends up laughing and having a beer with his colleagues afterwards. Dave's social abilities are easily overlooked, but reign supreme.

The fact that Dave gets my puns is a bonus. The fact that it took me forty-seven years to meet him is not. The fact that he loves and accepts me exactly the way that I am is priceless.

I don't know if Dave would have made it through my initial screening process, but I know that he would have loved chatting with me in a pumpkin costume.

Meg Ryan met Dennis Quaid making *DOA*; maybe Freud didn't work out so well for her either. The movie title should have been a clue.

✳ ✳ ✳

I'm not a big believer in past lives but if anything was going to allow me to give credence to the idea it would be downhill skiing. A previous life clearly ended in some catastrophic manner on an icy peak. I have a purely visceral response to the mere thought of standing atop a hill covered with powder: my heart pounds in my throat, my legs feel weak, and my hands start to shake.

I enjoy very little about the entire process. Getting ski boots on in the chalet is a challenge in and of itself. Those boot clasps are designed to humiliate the weak-fingered. Downhill boots are the foot version of a corset – stiff, unrelenting, cumbersome, and impossible to walk in gracefully.

Focus, Jackie. You've got this, Jackie. Heel, toe. Heel, toe. Ignore the cretins rolling their eyes behind you as you inch your way forward towards that lodge door. Time waits for no man, you say?

How about a woman? It can damn well wait for you.

Next come the god-awful concrete stairs. Step sideways, Jackie. One step at a time, Jackie. Grasp the rail. Stop crying, Jackie. And then there is the never-ending trek towards the base of the hill.

I have clomped my way along in said manner more times than I care to admit. I'm easily overtaken by Nordic gods and goddesses around me, strolling effortlessly by with their skis tossed jauntily over their shoulders, chic toques atop their heads, the epitome of cool. Who in the hell can stroll in a foot corset?

All of this just to get to the chairlift.

Oh, the chairlift. Another creation designed to humiliate and torture those less Lindsay Vonn and more Lucy Ricardo. It's all about the timing, evidently. Catching the lift seems to me to be like jumping into a double Dutch game. You watch the rope, wait for your moment, then go. Hesitate a split second and you've missed your chance.

If you should be lucky enough, you make it into perfect position just in the nick of time. The chair whizzing by catches you behind your knees, and you find yourself firmly plunked down upon a cold, hard, metal seat. Then the balance shuffle game begins. Oh, the shame should your side teeter down farther than that of the rotund, portly

gentleman's beside you. "It must be all that pou-
tine I had for lunch. Darn Québécois!" you weakly
joke.

Reality hits as you realize that only one tiny bar
lies between you and the vast chasm below. Your
clamouring heart steadies as you firmly clutch that
tiny bar and try to look around and enjoy the vista.
The lift shimmies, shakes, and then stalls as you try
not to think about plummeting to your death.

Then peace fills your heart as you realize that
you've got this. You are ascending a mountain. No
one can tell you apart from the rest of the uber-con-
fident people laughing and chatting in the air. You
are a skier, a member of the club. Strains of Sia's
"Titanium" filter through your brain. Thoughts of
owning a chalet flit through your head: ski in/ski
out? Two bedrooms? Gas or log?

You are mentally designing the great room when
suddenly there's a sign telling you to: LIFT BAR
HERE.

LIFT BAR HERE? Why no, thank you very
much. I believe I shall just carry on, now that I
have nailed chairlift riding, and take this baby all
the way back down. No one can stop me.

Apparently, someone can.

"Just stand. Let the chair push you gently. Veer
your skis to the right/left. Glide over to the side."

Glide. Right.

God forbid you fall. Should you fall, THE LIFT WILL STOP AND EVERY SINGLE PERSON ON THE FACE OF THE PLANET will stare at you. They will stare at you as you wrestle yourself, your poles, and your crisscrossed skis into some semblance of two-legged balance. They will continue to stare as you let out a halfhearted chuckle and a tremulous, "I've got it now!" to the crowd and slowly shuffle out of the way.

All of this just to make it to the top of the freakin' hill.

You might think, and justifiably so, from this recount that I am a novice skier. You would, however, be mistaken.

I have had (count 'em) three full days of lessons and hurtled down hills at six different ski resorts including one in Davos, Switzerland (another story for another day involving gondolas, snowstorms, and skiing blind).

My sister Lisa, aware of my previous experience, asked Dave and I to ski with her and Richard. We rendezvoused at the top of the baby hill with the intent of taking the next lift to the blue and black runs. When I made it clear that my intent was slightly different and that I was standing at my final destination, Lisa looked at me in confusion. Confusion grew to frustration as she looked around at the flailing beginners and finally begged,

"Jackie, tell me you're better than this."

I was not, in fact, better than this. I probably should have made this clear before agreeing to spend the day skiing with them.

Here's the thing: I knew by then that I did not like skiing. I knew that I was petrified of skiing. I had given it the good old college try multiple times and the verdict was in:

skiing + Jackie = misery and abject terror.

And yet …

Gentlemen beckoned. Several nice men tried in vain to make skiing a pleasurable pastime. Some pushed, some cajoled, and others quietly hoped, but all loved the sport and just wanted me to enjoy it with them.

And I said yes. That's on me.

I learned that I'm a terrific après-ski kind of girl. I will happily read my book in the hot tub while Dave skis and then meet him for a Baileys on ice by a crackling fire in a chalet.

It's a win-win.

Finally.

LIFE LESSON #2

CHOOSE PEOPLE WHO VALUE YOU EXACTLY THE WAY YOU ARE.

Try new things, be open to new experiences, but don't do things you truly dislike merely to make someone else happy. People need to accept you just the way you are, and you need the strength of character to put your foot down sometimes. Be exactly yourself, and that should be enough.

Maya Angelou pronounced, "When someone shows you who they are, believe them the first time."

If they love fastidious people who can shred mountains, that's awesome. Just don't try to mold anyone into being someone they're not. Don't go into a relationship hoping that your partner will change. We all do it to some extent. We think, "Oh, but if only he …" or "I'm sure she'll grow to like …" or "I know that if I could just get him to try …" Nope. Take off those rose-coloured glasses and see the person standing in front of you, warts and all, and decide if this is a person you want to be with. Focus on the reality, not the potential.

People-pleasers like myself struggle with saying no. We want to be the fun-loving, up-for-anything, go-along-with-it kind of girl. But we must be brave enough to present our true selves to the world; otherwise someone is going to want to return what they have with a "not as advertised" sign on it.

Hobbies and interests are just the tip of the iceberg. Family ties, behaviour under stress, personality types, addictions ... the list goes on. People can change and do change but only if and when *they* want to. Life's too short to bend yourself into a pretzel trying to be something you're not. I've been just as guilty in the past of expecting partners to change to fit my idealized version of acceptable. It never works out well for anyone.

Fred Rogers stated it best: "Love isn't a state of perfect caring. It is an active noun like struggle. To love someone is to strive to accept that person exactly the way he or she is, right here and now."

Now that's a neighbourhood I want to live in.

CHAPTER THREE

FIVE HUNDRED MILES

'm a "go-the extra-mile" kind of girl. I've been known to go all-out for birthday and Christmas presents, spending hour upon hour thinking about the perfect gift for someone I love. I have also literally gone the extra mile in the past for members of the opposite sex.

Growing up, we used to spend a couple of weeks every summer at my aunt and uncle's cottage. It was the highlight of our yearly school break and all four of us would tell you that those weeks were some of the happiest of our childhood. I recall lying in bed at night listening to the adults playing rousing games of euchre, sounds of Billy Joel blasting on the eight-track player (I still can't listen to "You May be Right" without being instantly transported to the cottage). My dad and uncle would prep for their yearly running race, and my mom and aunt trained just enough to justify eating Cheezies at night (on the "Hilly" road: walk up the hills/ run down the hills). We learned to swim off the dock, and explored the woods and fields around the cottage. I loved seeing my otherwise nonathletic mom slalom ski (water skiing on one ski) like she was born in the water, and watching the men battle it out on the tennis court. We barbecued on the mammoth, old-fashioned outdoor coal stove, after visiting Farmer Brown's to get fresh vegetables for supper. My cousins, siblings and I climbed the creatively named "Climbing Tree," and whiled away rainy days playing card games and creating card houses. We swam out to the island, following behind the canoe that had a dangling rope attached if we grew tired and needed to hitch a ride.

So many happy memories. The property was large and not only housed a cottage with four bedrooms, a living room, a kitchen, and a dining room, but also a boathouse. The boathouse was the dream. It was home to one motorboat, one sailboat, a canoe, and some nefarious turtles. The upper level featured an enormous furnished room that was surrounded on all four sides by a deck. It was white, and you could see it from the highway. "I see the boathouse!" was the refrain that always heralded our imminent arrival. That boathouse was our haven.

There were three boys.

The cottage two doors down belonged to a boy named Donald. Donald was friends with Blake, who was several doors down from him, and they were both friends with Shawn, who had a cottage down the road and up the hill. I had seen the boys off and on over the years, but the summer after grade eight was when I first truly SAW them.

They would ride by in their aluminum putt-putt boat with its 6.5 horsepower engine. I would wave idly from the lounge chair on the stone deck, ensuring that I was strategically positioned in my new red, one-piece bathing suit. That summer, my younger cousin Sally, Doug, and I spent hours with the boys. We explored the lake and the fields and indulged in game after game of hearts. My first kiss was a furtive, chaste one that happened at the end of that summer in the boathouse as my parents were packing the car.

Shawn. Oh, Shawn. Be still my beating heart.

The next summer, tragedy struck. The cottage was sold, and my aunt and uncle bought another one about a twenty-minute drive away. It was an even bigger cottage on an even bigger lot that also had a guest cottage on the property. It was beautiful, but it had no Blake, no Donald, and no Shawn. Sally and I spent days reminiscing about the boys and scheming up ways to see them again.

I am five years older than Sally. I've always thought of her as my equal and my friend, but really, looking back now, I cannot believe that I led my little cousin astray, because yes, yes, I did.

We came up with the ingenious idea of waking up early, packing a lunch, leaving a note (not specifying where we were going), and walking to the former lake. We travelled close to twenty-three kilometres. It was a hot summer day, and the vast majority of the walk was alongside a highway. (Do not leave me in charge of the care of your children—oh, wait.)

We walked and walked for hours and finally made it to the end of the Hilly Road. We were a paltry five-minute stroll away from Donald and Blake when a car pulled up beside us. It was our grandmother. The adults were out looking for us. Nanny told us to jump in, turned around, and that was that—no discussion or debate. Frustrated is too small of a word to express how we felt. Heartbroken, maybe? So close and yet so far.

We never saw the boys again.

Over the years to come, many boys would make my heart beat faster, but I don't know if I ever felt as bold and in charge of my own destiny as I did that sunny day walking the extra miles down Highway 35 towards Blake, Donald, and Shawn.

✶ ✶ ✶

I love that I can be spontaneous and dive headfirst into new adventures and experiences. I just wish that I was better at checking the depth of the water before diving.

I was in second-year university in London, Ontario, it was a Wednesday, and it was my birthday. Waiting tables at a small diner that evening with ten minutes left on my shift, it was just about time to close for the night. I was tired, my feet hurt, and I had an essay due the next day that still needed editing.

As I was scrubbing down a countertop, I heard a voice behind me asking for a cup of coffee. My heart sank. This meant that I had to get a new carafe going and the odds of getting out on the dot of nine would be nil. I turned around, plastered a smile on my face, only to see my boyfriend Ted. He was attending university in Guelph, Ontario, at the time. A friend of his had to come to London for a couple of hours that evening and he had hitched a ride to surprise me.

I was ecstatic. So romantic. What a gesture. We

went back to the house I shared with my room-mates and hung out for an hour or so before his ride was heading back to Guelph. Caught up in a romantic, movie-genre moment, I impulsively decided that I would go back with him, stay the night, and take the hour-and-a-half-long train ride back to London in the morning.

Lauren Bacall believed that a planned life was a dead life, and I took this to heart.

We made it to Guelph shortly after midnight.

The next morning, reality hit. My handwritten, still-to-be-edited essay was due by noon and my mother and sister were driving two hours to Lon-don to take me out for a birthday lunch shortly thereafter.

Apart from money for my train ticket, I had no extra cash or credit cards. I hopped on the train and settled in. I would arrive just in time to get back to my house, run in my essay, and meet the ladies. I was living life on the edge! I felt vibrant and alive and reveled in my spontaneity …

… until my unobservant nature proved to be a worthy adversary. I daydreamed and stared idly out the window for the first half of the journey before finally realizing with sickening clarity that this train was destined for Toronto, not London. The opposite direction.

East. West. They both end in "st."

In desperation, I told my sad story to anyone who would listen: the ticket master, the ticket master at the train station, the cleaner on the platform, the elderly gentlemen snoring beside me, the mom and son by the phone booth.

The lovely cleaner gave me a quarter and I made a collect call to my house in London where my mom and sister had just arrived. My figurative tail was between my legs as I meekly explained, "Hey! Guess what? Funny story!" They were unamused.

My mom spoke to the ticket master, gave him her credit card number, and paid for my new ticket to London.

I did not, in fact, get my essay in on time. Nor did I get my birthday lunch. I did, however, provide my family and friends with yet another Jackie story for years to come.

The following September, I switched schools. I transferred to Guelph University.

To be with Ted.

We broke up.

Don't switch schools for a boy. Or a girl.

But always check the depth of the water.

✷ ✷ ✷

Can men and women just be friends? Not if they spend a lot of time alone together. Eventually, at least in my experience, one or the other develops romantic feelings, and things get messy.

I was close friends for many years with Steve. Oh, Steve – my younger Achilles heel. We never dated, despite many a flirtatious exchange, but I held out hope for ages. I was sure that he would suddenly realize I was The One. He would see me in a more serious light, music would play, and credits would roll. I blame this on my high school English teacher, who told us the story of how she and her husband were just friends for years until, right after university, he suddenly "saw" her, and all her romantic hopes and dreams came to fruition.

She turned out to be the exception. Not the rule.

When I went off to teach in Kuwait, I said goodbye to Steve in my head and decided it was time to let go of the fantasy. I slung my metaphorical hobo stick over my shoulder, filled with hopes and dreams of a new adventure, and relinquished all thoughts of Stackie or Jeve. (I should have known it was doomed from the awkward meshing of our names.)

Life went on and I was happy. One day I was teaching in my classroom when the office buzzed to tell me that someone was there to see me. A young gentleman from my hometown had flown all the way over to Kuwait to surprise me and wanted to take me out to dinner.

My God. Could it be? Was it possible? Steve had seen the light? How was my hair?

Cue montage as I raced towards the office in slow-mo. Forgotten memories of the two of us slow dancing, driving down the highway together, and laughing in the snow filled the screen in my head. Harry ran through New York City to make it to Sally before the ball dropped. Clearly Steve had flown around the globe to start his life as soon as possible too.

I spun around the last corner on winged feet, flew into the office and ... stopped short. Yes, there was a man waiting there, and no, it wasn't Steve. I'd never seen him before in my life.

Euphoria died a quick death.

It turns out that my visitor was the son of an acquaintance of my mom. She and Mom had gotten to chatting and she mentioned that her son would be going to Kuwait in a military role. Mom had given her my address and suggested that he look me up.

It would have made for an excellent rom-com if Military Boy and I had gone out for dinner, fallen in love and run off into the desert with the blazing sun setting behind us, but it was not to be.

He did invite me for dinner, but only had that evening free. I was hosting a party and explained that I couldn't go but invited him to join the fun.

He became indignant and left—five minutes after my breathless flight towards the rest of my life.

Steve was a great guy who cared about me, but not quite enough in the end. I've been both the Friend Zonee and the Friend Zoner in life and neither is fun. Sometimes, as painful as it can be, that's the way the cookie crumbles.

Romantic comedies should come with a warning: may cause unrealistic dating expectations; consult a therapist if symptoms appear.

LIFE LESSON #3

GO THE EXTRA MILE BUT KNOW WHEN IT'S TIME TO STOP WALKING.

Grand gestures are laudable. They are romantic and cinematic and can stir the heart like no other. If you want to make a grand gesture for someone that you love, go for it. Just know that it may not be reciprocated. Grand gestures might not be your partner's currency.

Dave makes me tea every morning that he's here. Exactly the way that I like it by the time I roll out of bed. It's a little gesture in lots of ways but speaks volumes to me about his feelings.

Actions don't have to always be quid pro quo and rarely will be in a relationship. Sometimes you'll be giving a solid eighty percent and your partner will be barely able to scrape up twenty. Life gets busy and stressful, and you can't give your full energy to everything at the same time. The trick is finding someone who will be willing to put in that eighty percent when you can hardly muster your share. It's a balancing act. Sometimes you're both at a ten and that's when you really need to tread carefully.

Be especially kind to each other when that happens.

Walk all day down a highway, hop on that train, and fly across the country to surprise the person that you love. It makes life exciting. Just make sure that it's not all one-sided. If someone's not that into you, then it's time to look elsewhere (or even nowhere—being single is ridiculously underrated).

This goes both ways, of course. I have stayed too long at the party with guys that I knew, deep down, weren't right for me, but I didn't want to hurt them. Life is short. Do each other a favour and move on.

Ah, men. The bane of my existence. I once asked my mother to guess my least likely career path (thinking she would say house cleaner), and her answer was, "A nun."

I don't think she was referring to my lack of religious fervour.

I've learned a lot about relationships in my life but still feel like a mere beginner. What I have learned, though, is actually simple and can be summed up in a few lines:

* Choose a best friend that you like having sex with (and have a fair bit of it).

* Fight fair – no character attacks, focus on the issue at hand. As Michael J. Fox says, "Talk like you like each other," because hopefully you do. The

goal isn't to win; the goal is to solve a problem.

* Be happy yourself—that's not in anyone else's job description.

There is nothing earth-shattering here, nothing that most people don't already know. Things like values, respect, honesty, having fun together, et cetera are clearly important too, but hopefully they would be covered in #1. It's hard to be best friends with someone if you don't have those.

My sister-in-law Karen says that Doug has every quality she was searching for in a partner. They're one of the best-suited couples I know, so being clear on what you are looking for is probably a good thing too.

Friends of mine have been a couple since the beginning of grade eight and they're still happy. Maybe there's also an element of luck involved (or else they were just super-pickers at the age of thirteen).

Mostly, get your own house in order. Then you're good if you meet the right person, and you're good on your own if you don't.

CHAPTER FOUR

A ROLLING STONE

*L*ike taxes and death, the unpredictability of life is one of the few things you can count on. A curveball will come at you when you least expect it, and when it does you need to catch it and dribble (I'm a die-hard Raptors fan, so I can't bring myself to say "hit it out of the park"). There have been many times that I have been taken by surprise and caught off guard, but have had to put on my game face, shrug, and go with it.

* * *

Getting a teaching job at an American international school in Kuwait months after the end of the Gulf War was unsurprisingly easy. Shockingly, the competition wasn't too stiff. By the time I had seen the job ad, interviewed, obtained my first-ever passport, and booked a flight, school had already started.

A three-hour drive to the airport in Toronto, a flight to Heathrow, a frenzied race around the airport dealing with visa issues, and then the plane ride to Kuwait had made for a rather long day.

Jared and I introduced ourselves at the airport and flew out of Canada together. We became close friends during my Middle Eastern years, and then, many years and a divorce later, dated. His immutable ability to provide levity made even the mad scramble to sort out visa issues at Heathrow (and frankly, everything else in life) fun.

Our plane landed in Kuwait City at two in the morning and we were met by the high school principal. Upon dropping us off at our apartments, he kindly let us know that we could take the 6:30 or 7:00 a.m. bus to school in the morning for our introduction day. I blearily replied that the latter bus sounded good to me and staggered to my room, two suitcases in tow. Trying to pack for a whole year, including all my freshly acquired school supplies to use for the grade three class I would be teaching, had been a challenge. These days I need two bags for a mere overnight.

The next morning, buoyed by excitement (oh, to be youthful and able to jump time zones so readily), I had my first tour of the school. My head was reeling at the sight of bullet holes in the office couch and at the state of the library, with dusty books in giant piles all over the floor. The school had been used as an interrogation centre during the war, and the evidence of that was daunting.

As we finished our tour, the principal stopped outside of a kindergarten room. I heard the students inside and smiled dutifully, waiting to head back to the grade three wing and peek inside my soon-to-be classroom. Just then the door flew open; a woman literally ran out, high-fived the principal, and I was ever-so-gently ushered in. A secretary had been covering the class until the new teacher arrived.

I was the new teacher.

Not grade three. Junior kindergarten. Not starting tomorrow. Right now.

Within seconds the door closed behind me as the principal wisely did a drop-and-run, and I was left staring at the myriad faces before me. Kindergarten. *Very* minimal English. No supplies. No time to prepare. They stared at me, and I stared at them. The showdown lasted just a few seconds before they, clearly realizing I was no threat, resumed their frenetic racing around the classroom.

Frozen for a minute or two, my tired brain tried to process this new reality. Then, giving myself a mental, "Roll with it, Jackie," I dove in, calling out a very quiet, "Cover me!" for my own amusement.

Masking tape is a godsend. It's a miracle what a circle on the floor can do to a group of unruly four-year-olds. Add in a few songs with actions and, despite the inauspicious beginning, sanity was restored.

As the year progressed, I grew to love teaching my sweet ruffians and became attached to them. I will never forget seeing some of them dive under their chairs during a storm as they mistook a clap of thunder for the sound of a detonating bomb. One boy's father was missing; he had been taken as a human shield and hadn't been seen since. The aftermath of the war was evident daily, and I took solace in the fact that I was able to provide a little TLC to my children each day.

I learned a lot over the course of the year— probably more from them than they learned from newbie me. I'm glad that I didn't turn tail and run that first day when I was unwittingly tossed into the deep end.

✳ ✳ ✳

"When in Rome" became my mantra during a 1994 visit to a spa in Baden Baden. I had stopped off for a vacation in Germany on the way home from Kuwait one summer with my then-boyfriend Ron. Visiting the Black Forest was a real treat; it was stunning and majestic with meticulously maintained homes. Verdant green meadows, towering evergreens and breathtaking waterfalls made it a truly awe-inspiring sight.

Baden Baden, at the edge of the area, housed many spas that beckoned, and we decided that we couldn't pass by without stopping for a day of self-indulgence. It was my first foray into the decadent world of luxury treatments. Our destination was the one-hundred-plus-year-old Friedrichsbad Spa. The opulence of the building took my breath away.

We soon learned that there were seventeen different stations, with steam rooms, hot dry air, and thermal baths of varying temperatures that you moved through with showers in between. Ron and I parted ways after entering and I made my way towards the first women's station.

Clothing of any sort appeared to be *verboten*.

This was novel. My half-assed, puritan Canadian sensibilities took pause for a moment.

Mental shrug.

As I made my way around the spas, my self-consciousness gradually abated, and I reveled in the experience. I felt peaceful and frankly rather

European by the time I entered Station 11, the pool.

I strolled out, au naturel, confident, with an "I Am Woman Hear Me Roar" sway, until suddenly, I froze. A deer-in-the-headlights look quickly replaced my avant-garde demeanour.

Men were there. Utterly naked men of all shapes and sizes intermingled with utterly naked women of all shapes and sizes. (Forgive me for my candidness, but I must mention seeing the most profoundly large pair of testicles one could ever imagine. I mean, these suckers were huge. They scarred me for life and were forever burned on my brain. Now they've scarred you, too. You're welcome.)

We weren't in Kansas, Toto.

No maidenly shriek left my body. Instead, I lifted my chin, and regally made my way into the throngs. Nerves of steel, I say.

I eventually completed the stations and left feeling entirely relaxed and rather proud of myself for letting it all hang out.

So cosmopolitan.

My cousin Kathryn, who lived in Germany for years, later told me that I probably just missed the sign outside the first station stating in German: Robes, 2 Deutsche Marks.

✳ ✳ ✳

I have hopped, skipped, and jumped around the world in various teaching roles in a variety of schools (both private and public) since I was twenty-three. A brief stint with the Children's Aid Society and two maternity leaves aside, I have been a teacher's aide, a teacher-in-training, a substitute teacher, or an elementary teacher for more than thirty years. Over the course of those years, I have had many moments of, "Keep your game face on, Jackie, and go with it."

Teachers everywhere know that nothing is sacred when it comes to kids. Every state secret gets spilled in the elementary classroom—especially in the primary grades. When these moments come up, the urge to cover my ears is strong, but the urge to dart outside and laugh until my stomach hurts or I pee a little is even stronger.

Supply teaching (substituting) at a public school in a rougher area of Ottawa after returning from life overseas kept me busy. Introducing a unit on money to a grade two class was a walk in the park and, although I had never been in that classroom before, I was feeling confident. Three minutes into the lesson, my confidence was shaken when a little girl jumped up suddenly and called out, "Money? My daddy makes lots of money!"

I chuckled a little and made some noncommittal remarks while taking a mental note to find out what he did (sign me up). She then continued, spreading her arms out wide, "He has a big machine, a BIIIIIG machine in the basement that always makes money. It just keeps coming out. We're rich, rich, rich!"

Unless you're Kate Moss, it's difficult to pull off stripes, so I decided that discretion was the better part of valour and didn't sign up.

Reading Jan Brett's illustrated storybook *The Mitten* to a grade one class was a lesson that I always enjoyed. We had a giant cloth floor mitten and animal masks for the children to help them reenact the process of trying to find a space in which to stay warm throughout the cold winter. Halfway through the reading one year, a little boy piped up and confided, "My mommy and daddy had a big fight last night and Daddy slept on the couch!"

I valiantly tried to steer the conversation back to the fox and the mole and the badger, but it was too late. The avalanche had begun.

"My daddy sleeps on the couch A LOT!"

"One time, my daddy slept on the couch and Mommy threw water on him!"

"My daddy can't cook eggs right and they got in a big fight this morning. Maybe he'll sleep on the couch tonight."

Who knew there was so much couch-surfing going on? And always the dads? What happened to equality?

I am keenly aware that teachers of my own children have probably heard far more than I would like about my own life, too. That's just the nature of the beast. No filter.

"Ms. Ewing, my penis has poop on the end of it! Why is there poop on my penis, Ms. Ewing?"

"Why are you so old, Ms. Ewing? My grandma thinks you taught her. Did you teach her when you weren't old?"

"Can I rub your legs, Ms. Ewing? *Please* let me rub your legs." Note to self: don't wear skirts, especially during story time on the carpet.

"Ms. Ewing, I love you more than Colonel Sanders loves lickin' chicken!"

Sometimes it's not the kids who have me struggling to keep a straight face, it's the parents.

From a real parent-teacher interview:

"My son is possessed. I'm sure you've noticed."

Umm, possessed? No, no, I can't say as I have.

"Keep an eye out for the elderly woman with a deep voice or the high-pitched two-year-old to come through. Please keep us posted; it's becoming an issue."

And sometimes it's the staff.

The door burst open into my grade 3/4

classroom and my principal strode in, waving her hands in the air. "Sex! Sex! Sex! Am I just supposed to have sex with THE SAME MAN, YEAR AFTER YEAR, FOR THE REST OF MY LIFE?"

Why yes, yes you are; it's actually called marriage. But hey—whatever works; no judgment here. Can we move this conversation to the hall though, please?

And sometimes you just have to shake your head. About halfway through the fall one year, a new student joined my third-grade classroom in Kuwait. He was sweet, nervous, and cheerful. He shyly asked to go to the washroom on his first day. When a lot of time had passed, and he hadn't returned, I sent the cavalry out to search for him. He was thankfully where he said he would be—in the bathroom. Pants around his ankles. Standing. Waiting. He was waiting ... for the maid to come and pull up his pants. The maid wasn't enrolled in our elementary school, so the poor kid had a steep learning curve ahead of him. He got two brand spanking new Jet Skis for his ninth birthday, though. They were blue. He was happy.

The things they don't teach you in teacher's college.

✳ ✳ ✳

As a newlywed teacher living in Monterrey, Mexico, life was pretty good. I loved my class and job at an American international school. My new husband Mike and I lived in a spacious apartment on the edge of the Sierra Madre mountain range. The school was enormous, with anywhere from six to eight classes of each grade level, and hallways opened onto courtyards resplendent with greenery. The staff were a very hardworking group. I remember attending one staff meeting where a few teachers brought up the problem of the guard dogs scaring them at midnight. My face clearly expressed my "maybe the problem is that you're still at school at midnight" thought.

I didn't speak the language but quickly learned how to order a *Quarter Pounder con queso, nada más, por favor*. I enjoyed some low-key hikes and exploring the area, which was a playground for outdoor enthusiasts (or an American Ninja Warrior course for out-of-shape tea grannies like me).

The parent community was strong—welcoming and accommodating to those from another country trying to acclimatize. One weekend, a family from Mike's class invited us to visit their ranch. It was a beautifully warm day and we spent it hiking, picnicking, and exploring a water-filled cave that was chock-full of bats hanging inches above our heads. I was feeling adventurous and rugged as we jumped into the jeep to head back at the end of the outing.

Suddenly the jeep jerked to a halt, the father jumped out, shouted a few things in Spanish, grabbed a rock, and ... bashed a rattlesnake on the head until it died. All of this happened in seconds. Apparently, rattlesnakes were a menace to the cattle on his land.

Minutes later, snake in a bag on top of the jeep, blood trickling down onto the windshield, we were on our way again. Mike and I were back at their home and saying our goodbyes when they kindly offered us a parting gift: the snake. It would make for a mouthwatering supper, we were told. The blood would wash right off: Just skin, clean, and *"devorar"*!

Claro que sí.

Polite facial features stoically in place, we thanked them profusely and headed home.

Many years later, our children, Molly and Finn, would become die-hard fans of the television show *Survivor*. Being handed a huge, freshly-killed snake to eat would have been like a five-course meal to the contestants. Maybe I just needed to starve myself first.

The snake went into the fridge for the evening. Who knew that bagged, headless, refrigerated rattlesnake could jump? Reaching in to grab my cold Diet Coke was a traumatizing, but nevertheless necessary experience.

The next day we proceeded to skin Snakey on our balcony. It was one long sucker and standing on a chair was required.

I am Jackie and I have skinned a rattlesnake. Well, co-skinned.

Roar.

We kept the rattle for many years to come. It came in handy during science lessons and one-upping students during show-and-tell.

We did end up cooking the poor fellow in the end.

FYI: It didn't taste remotely like chicken.

***

Although I am usually able to roll with challenges, Covid-19 has tested my limits, and sometimes I have failed miserably.

Between the two of us, Dave and I have four children, and they range in age from seventeen to twenty-one. With the shutdown of universities, schools, and businesses, we had to endure many months of constant togetherness. I love my family dearly, but being progressively more introverted in my old age, I was desperately seeking space. I had switched to part-time teaching during Covid, so was home during the day more than normal—even when schools were open.

My perpetually cheerful husband was working from home at the corner desk in our open-concept living room/kitchen/dining room. He enjoyed looking out the windows at the birds while he worked and being in the thick of things with the family, so was more than okay with his spot. The kids spent one week with us and one week with their other parents, and some other spaces were available fifty percent of the time.

I gently suggested a few times that the two downstairs bedrooms were vacant and that maybe he could move down there during the weeks the kids were gone as a compromise. Happy wife = happy life and all that. This would free up access to the kitchen and the living room during the day. Dave's day started by seven and often didn't end until five, so it made for a lot of tiptoeing around, especially given the fact that he was on calls most of the time.

Eventually, we (the royal "we") agreed that he would give it a try when the kids were gone. Project Save Jackie's Sanity was on, and Day One was marked on my mental calendar in all caps. I floated home from school that first day at 12:10 p.m. feeling like it was Christmas morning. Oh, the anticipation! The kitchen/living room would be mine for a few precious hours! Peace! Solitude! Space! Halle-frickin-lujah! Diet Coke and a good book on the couch beckoned.

My commute was a three-minute walk, but what a glorious three minutes it was. Almost orgasmic.

I took a breath and opened the front door and stepped into my nirvana.

Except…

The TV was on—loudly. The radio was on—loudly. Rosie the Roomba was roaming – loudly and Dave was pacing the living room, talking animatedly on the phone.

In Dave's retelling of the story, I stood still, door ajar, hand on hip, frozen in place for a moment and then spat out with a shrewish bark, "When I'm here, could you not be?"

I submit that I did not utter those words but concede that the implication was quite possibly there.

After almost a year of intermittent lockdowns, I had nothing left. No roll with it. No game face. Nothing. Clearly, I can't always just go with it.

Dave moved his office into the basement that day. We're still married.

✳ ✳ ✳

I like wheat. I like it a lot. Toasted cinnamon-raisin bagels for breakfast. Crusty French baguettes with ham and cheese for lunch. Homemade macaroni and cheese for supper.

Divine.

Until my body decided to play a callous trick on me and decided that, in my early forties, it had had enough of wheat, spelt, rye, and barley ... "Oh no," it said. "I am done. Gluten, be gone."

It took a while for me to translate my body's language and figure out why my stomach was blowing up like a balloon every day. I started going to the secondhand shops and buying maternity wear and XXL tops to disguise my hideous bloat.

Tests were run, and scary things were ruled out before a friend suggested I try cutting out gluten. Lo and behold, all bloating stopped. Giant attire became cleaning rags.

Pivot.

As much as I loved my glutenous products, I learned to live without a lot of them, and over time, restaurants and stores started providing options that I could substitute. Candies, processed foods, and much fast food stopped making their way into my life, and I adjusted.

If only Ruffles chips had gluten in them. I'd be

a Jackie-twig.

One day at school, a fellow teacher, Greta, told the staff that she had baked a special pie from scratch to share. It was even gluten-free, she announced. Greta is a soul-sister of a woman—the kind that shoves her Christmas tree, fully decorated, into the storage room every January to be easily hauled out and plunked in the living room the following December. She was not naturally a Betty Crocker kind of girl, so she was very proud of her home-baked offering.

I happily partook in a slice of pie, and yes, it was delicious. A masterpiece. Until, a brief ten minutes later, my stomach spoke loudly and vociferously: reject, reject!

I raced down to Greta's classroom and said, "Tell me the truth! Did you really make this from scratch?"

She indignantly replied, "I did! I got the recipe from my sister and made the lemon filling myself. It's gluten-free!"

And then I asked about the crust. It took a few weak denials before Greta fessed up that it was indeed premade. She was horrified when she realized (i.e., saw) what this meant for me.

Grabbing an oversized cardigan to cover myself, I covertly made my way to the principal's office. Barging in, I stood in front of his desk and flung open the sweater. "Look at me," I spit out. "I am *not* standing up in front of grade sevens and eights like this!" My swollen belly now resembled that of a distinctly pregnant lady. Eyes bulging, mouth agape, and clearly flummoxed, the principal hastily agreed to cover my class and sent me home.

Staff meetings were entertaining from then on. My principal and fellow staff members would teasingly suggest a meatball or donut as snacks were passed around the table. Offers to put the camera on my stomach with bets on how quickly I could blow up became a regular thing. Real money changed hands.

Fun times.

I'm very cautious now. I've had a lot of years to play with my limits and know that there's very little wiggle room on my gluten-free diet.

The dinner guest from hell.

✳ ✳ ✳

Sometimes just going with it helps others. My friend Sue and I were invited to be dates at a military ball one year. Decked out in gorgeous dresses, with shoes, hair, and makeup befitting Cinderella—post Fairy Godmother intervention—we met our princes and headed to the event. Great food, music, and company were the hallmarks of the evening.

As Sue and I exited the ladies' room, all freshened up halfway through the night, two handsome, unfamiliar young men resplendent in their crimson military garb were waiting for us. They introduced themselves, apologized for being stalkers, and explained that they hoped we would take pity on them. Could we give them a hand? Their parents had been told that their sons were escorting female dates to the ball. Pictures were required to send home to doting moms and dads; stand-ins were needed.

We squeezed four hours into fifteen minutes that night.

Clinking glasses. *Flash.* Dipping on the dance floor. *Flash.* Eating shrimp on a skewer. *Flash.* Boogying to Bob Seger. *Flash.* Arms around each other on a couch. *Flash.* Jazz hands flapping as we made funny faces. *Flash. Flash. Flash.*

Broad smiles on our faces at every snap. Frozen in time, stuffed into a shoebox in a basement somewhere, our montage of events proves that photographs are not always accurate chroniclers of history.

That night, going with the flow helped two young men put off uncomfortable conversations with their families that they weren't quite ready to have. And I'm cool with being a party to that.

✳ ✳ ✳

As a single mom on a tight budget, my friend Lynn was excited about her upcoming vacation to Mexico with her son Hayden. Plans were made well in advance, the resort thoroughly researched, new summer attire purchased, and bags packed.

Unfortunately, at the last minute a family illness caused them to cancel the trip. Lynn and Hayden were despondent and in need of cheering.

I rallied a young Finn and Molly together and we put surprise Operation Cheer Lynn and Hayden Up into motion: we would bring Mexico to them.

Beach towels, folding chairs, tubes of sunscreen, mariachi music, tiny little umbrellas for nonalcoholic mojitos and piña coladas, fixings for tacos, and of course the requisite piñata in hand, we descended upon them. The basement became a beachfront Riviera Maya.

It was a huge hit that would culminate in the pummeling of the piñata.

We all trooped upstairs and into their backyard. The piñata was hoisted up to a beam, strategically positioned at perfect batting level. Blindfolded one by one, the kids took turns attacking the bright pink horse with a determined vehemence.

They bludgeoned that piñata until they were as bright-faced as it was, but to no avail. A few mighty cracks from Lynn and I (okay, fine, it was Lynn), and a tiny opening was finally revealed. The kids went back to work. After another ten glorious minutes of hope, cheering, and whacking, the piñata, at long last, broke open.

The kids fell to the ground, their innocent eyes ablaze with joy. It was Christmas morning once again.

Three faces looked at the piñata. Three faces looked at the ground. Three faces looked at me.

Who knew that piñatas were sold empty?

The pinata was a sad, empty, desecrated vessel, swaying slowly in the breeze. A bird chirped obliviously in the distance and then ... silence.

Time froze. My life drifted before me in slow motion.

What seemed like an eternity passed until suddenly, thoughts of WWKD (What Would Karen Do) (Karen is highly adept at distracting her children during awkward moments) filled my head.

The words, "Who wants ice cream?" popped out as if of their own volition.

We all ended up going to the actual Riviera Maya together when the kids were much older. While a fun trip, I submit that it wasn't much better than our makeshift holiday that day in Lynn's basement.

***

I'm not usually big on public displays of affection. You won't catch me on the Kiss-Cam. No siree, Bob. My husband and I don't even dance around the kitchen when the kids are around (their vomiting sounds tend to put a damper on the moment). I was especially self-conscious in my teens.

If you're going to get a hickey, winter is the best time. Plan accordingly. Mark it on your calendar. Winter. Autumn works, too. Maybe even spring. But not summer.

I stealthily snuck up our flight of stairs one July night as a teen—carefully stretching my legs to bypass the odd wily, squeaky step. No lights came on, no parental voice rang out; I was home free.

Sitting on the padded bench at my vanity table, I inspected the damage. My first hickey and it was a doozy. I pondered methods of concealment. Foundation might work. Mock neck sleeveless tops, too. Staying in bed with the covers up to my chin, pleading stomach cramps for a week was always an option.

No one had to know. No one *would* know.

Satisfied with my clever little plan, I climbed into bed and, perhaps exhausted from my extracurricular excitement, fell immediately asleep. Only to be awakened a few hours later by an intense, throbbing pain in my index finger. A simple hang-nail had become infected and my finger was now bright red and two sizes larger than normal.

I staggered my way to the top of the staircase, ready to head down to the kitchen and our medicine cabinet, when a wave of dizziness overcame me. I reached out to steady myself by grabbing the newel post as I looked down at the long flight of stairs below me.

And then … well, then I fainted.

Never had I ever. Never have I ever since.

My timing in life is impeccable.

It turns out that I'm a highly talented fainter. Instead of plunging forwards down sixteen stairs, I conveniently fell sideways—into the glass-paned bookshelf that graced our hallway. One mere pane popped out neatly (that spot remains glassless to this day) as my head crashed into it. Small heads come in handy sometimes.

Although a directionally tidy fainter, I did not manage the feat silently. When I opened my eyes, lights blazed from every fixture and five faces stared at me from above. Initial looks of panic turned into Cheshire cat grins from my siblings; the heinous hickey was on full display.

Best-laid plans of mice, men, and Jackie very often go awry.

I ended up going to the hospital to stop the

quick-spreading infection. Volunteers, reception-
ists, doctors, nurses, fellow patients—my audience
was vast.

My parents never did say a single word to me
about my temporary neck tattoo. They didn't have
to.

Literally everyone else said it for them.

LIFE LESSON #4

ADAPT AND BE FLEXIBLE.

Whether it's something as major as adjusting to life alone in a new country or as minor as students catching you off guard, life is going to throw you a curveball or two. Being flexible and adaptable is a life skill worth cultivating. Things very rarely go as planned. Facing a (hopefully) once-in-a-lifetime global pandemic has tested limits worldwide in this regard.

Legendary basketball coach John Wooden taught his players that "flexibility is the key to stability," and I concur. If you can learn to manage the changes that come at you, you're less likely to be negatively affected by things out of your control. Being open-minded and willing to pivot and embrace new circumstances can only make life happier.

Fighting the current can be exhausting, but reframing the situation with a humorous lens helps. Taking a minute or two to deep-breathe does, too. I suspect meditation helps as well, although I've never quite gotten the hang of that. (As soon as I start visualizing myself in my happy place—sitting under a covered porch in the fall while it rains, gazing at the water—I start picturing what I'm wearing and then I'm down a fashion rabbit hole, meditation be damned.)

Mostly though, like anything else in life, practice makes perfect. The more you immerse yourself in new situations where you're likely to have novel experiences, the better you'll be at adapting on the fly. Turn and face the strange. Change is one of the few things that you can count on in life, so you might as well embrace it.

CHAPTER FIVE

LIVE A LITTLE

*I went to the woods because I wished to
live deliberately, to front only the essential facts
of life, and see if I could not learn what it had
to teach, and not, when I came to die, discover
that I had not lived.*

- HENRY DAVID THOREAU

L ife goes by in a heartbeat. I still feel the same
inside; it's only when I look in the mirror
that I am reminded I'm not in my thirties
anymore. The fact that sixty is the next milestone
for me is mind-boggling. I plan on living until I'm
one hundred and three, so I guess that I'm a little
more than halfway through the woods.

Sometimes I need a flashlight, sometimes a compass, and sometimes I get full-on lost and need to hug a tree until I'm found, but it's always an adventure.

✳ ✳ ✳

As a young girl, I was continually sick. All my report card comments seemed to start with, "Despite the number of days Jackie has missed due to illness …." In the '70s, there was very little to do when you were stuck at home, and so reading became my solace. I read and reread *Trixie Beldon*, *Nancy Drew*, the *Anne of Green Gables* series, *Little Women*, Beverly Cleary, Judy Blume, the *Little House on the Prairie* series, and *Heidi*. The list was endless. I was fortunate to have parents who modelled reading for joy and a host of novels in our home to keep me busy. (One summer, Karla was at the cottage with us on a rainy day, looked around and saw, as she says, "A Ewing in every corner reading a book." We all read.) I revelled in the stories. Daydreaming of future escapades became a pastime that would last a lifetime. This explains why my laundry is piled up, my house is messy, and I'm not too fond of the surprise drop-in visits.

Growing up in a small town, we had exactly one taxi and zero buses with which to get around.

Much to the amusement of my friends, I didn't even know how to get the bus to stop when I first rode one. Who knew that you had to pull on the thin, hanging rope thingy?

Little daydreaming Jackie who couldn't stop a bus would end up travelling all over the world, experiencing multiple adventures. I'm not even remotely physically intrepid (see also: ski story in Chapter Two) but I'm confident that you could plunk me down pretty much anywhere, in any gathering, town, city, or country on my own, and I would thrive.

Discovering that several teachers had walked out of a small school in Moosonee, Ontario at Christmas and that they were hiring was music to my unemployed (i.e., broke), newly graduated ears. I hadn't gone to teacher's college yet, but the unknown beckoned, and I answered the call. Sitting on that flight, in a tiny plane, I experienced absolute euphoria. I didn't know a soul and had no idea where I would be living, but the pure joy of going off into the unknown on my own was overpowering. I would experience that same feeling while flying solo to Kuwait and Scotland later in life as well. Had I known then that the same flight from Toronto to Moosonee a couple of weeks previously had resulted in a crash landing with another teacher on board, I might have been a tad more cautious in my outlook.

Moosonee is a town of about 1,300 in northern Ontario on the Moose River, just south of James Bay and is often called the Gateway to the Arctic. There were/are no roads into Moosonee and it's only accessible by plane or train so once you're there, you're really there. The average temperatures during the winter months are minus 14 to minus 30 degrees Celsius. During the winter, the Moose River was used as a road connecting Moose Factory and Moosonee, and spring breakup was a sight to behold.

I learned that flying south for March Break did not mean Florida, but rather the small, northern town of Timmons (population 42,000) and that eating out meant a singular, tiny town restaurant. Curling (running on ice—seriously, who came up with that idea?), snowmobiling, and hanging with the other teachers was our entertainment.

Dressed in my tall, white Sorel boots and my grandfather's old down-filled jacket (about three times too big), I loved going for walks. It was truly frosty, but when the sun was shining, and it often was, it was stunningly beautiful. The snow was pure white; what fell, stayed. After a while, I adjusted to the weather, although seeing the kids racing around at recess sometimes with hats and mitts tossed carelessly on the ground was still a bit of a shock. I never became that acclimatized.

Teaching was an eye-opener. I did not do my sixteen students justice; I had no clue how to plan and my kids paid the price. I grew especially attached to my grade two class, though, and can still picture their faces. Many of them had unfathomably tough lives and their resilience was awe-inspiring. One student had carried his younger brother's body home after he had been hit and killed by a rock thrown at his head. Another girl, I was told, had been raped by an older student. Several kids made it to school only if they woke themselves and their younger siblings up. The stories were endless and spoke volumes about our country's failure to do justice to our First Nations population. It's long past time to untangle the Gordian knot we've created.

At the end of that summer, I saw a job advertisement in the paper for a teaching position in Kuwait. The Gulf War had started in January 1991, and I had followed it in the news. It was officially over by the end of February, but the country had been ravaged by war and was left reeling in the aftermath.

Without the benefit of our good friend Google in those days, I was flying blind. I was put in touch with a Canadian girl who had taught there prewar and had loved it. She had travelled the world, met her husband, and collected a ton of 18-karat gold jewelry in the process. Flights to and from Kuwait were paid for, furnished housing was provided, utility bills covered, American and Kuwaiti holidays celebrated. Sign me up. I also credit my dad for this decision as one day, swinging on our porch swing, he encouraged me with, "Go for it, Jac." His was the lone voice in the wilderness, though, since everyone else thought I was crazy.

I will never forget flying into Kuwait City and seeing the oil fires burning from the air. Almost seven hundred wells had been set on fire by the Iraqi military, lasting from January until the final one was extinguished in November of '91. The country bore the aftermath of the fires in many ways.

So much vegetation had died. Everything was colorless. Beige sand, beige buildings ... it's no wonder I dreamed of walking down leafy sidewalks night after night for the first few weeks. Cockroaches were our constant household companions. During the months that buildings sat abandoned, they had moved right in, these roommates from hell. A cockroach crawling along my showerhead became a common sight. Soon I grew almost indifferent to the little beasts and casually smashed them with a hand weight as they scuttled by.

Walking along sand paths (ruined many a shoe), waking to the call to prayer, the odd sandstorm, and the blistering temperature took time to adjust to. One day in June, Jared fried an egg on the hood of his car. What I'm saying here is that it was hot.

Exploring the area with friends took us to the Highway of Death, a six-lane highway running between Kuwait and Iraq that was used by the Iraqis during the invasion. Over 60 miles of highway was littered with thousands of Iraqi cars, buses, and trucks and even some tanks.

Failaka Island was another day's exploration. Around two thousand residents had fled during the war, and the aftermath was evident everywhere we looked. Abandoned tanks, cars, and the detritus of everyday life—dolls, clothes, dishes—lay littered in plain sight.

The city arena had been used to store bodies during the war. When it eventually opened for public ice skating, we took advantage of an opportunity for some entertainment. Surprisingly, I was no better at skating on a rink in the desert than at home, and the Kuwaitis whizzing by put me to shame. I surreptitiously (albeit unpatriotically) hid my Canadian flag pinned to my jacket while cautiously shuffling around the ice.

Going to the beach was exciting; I still can't believe we did. It was deserted (shocker), and we could hear the occasional bomb detonating nearby. There were still Scud missiles in the sand where we swam so looking down in the clear water was highly recommended.

One night we went swimming in the Gulf with a few Green Berets. I expected them to arise from the water with knives gleaming between their teeth (I'd seen *First Blood*), but they presented as surprisingly normal, much to my chagrin.

Thanksgiving approached in early October, and we were told that Canadian soldiers weren't allowed to leave their base for the holiday unless invited to go somewhere. Many of us opened our homes to small groups of them for a home-cooked meal. I was shocked to realize just how exceedingly young so many soldiers were—just boys, really. Pimply and earnest and talking about their moms, girlfriends, and feeling lonely. I always think of them on Remembrance Day.

The captain of a group ended up at my apartment. As they prepared to leave, he thanked me profusely and asked if there was anything that they could do to show their appreciation. After pausing for a split second, I asked if they actually did march and sing, just like in the movies. Minutes later, I was the recipient of my very own private call-and-response cadence performance as the soldiers marched down the road in front of my apartment.

One weekend, a group of teachers went on a day's expedition to an island for some picnicking and swimming. Our driver started gesticulating on the way home, zipping along in a motorboat. In a mix of broken English and Arabic, we gleaned that he had spotted fins coming towards us. Dolphins—a pod of dolphins, and our boat was surrounded in minutes. The driver stopped the motor, and we sat in wordless silence as those breathtaking creatures put on the show of a lifetime, free of charge, in the Persian Gulf. Leaping, flipping, nudging each other and the boat—time seemed to stop. I awoke from my reverie when a fellow teacher suddenly stood up, jumped overboard and frolicked with those magnificent mammals. I will always regret not jumping in too. If I was granted a few do-over moments in my life, this would be one I would choose.

I stayed in Kuwait for five years. Throughout my travels, I found lifelong friends and met my first husband, resulting in two beautiful children. I am so grateful that I took a leap of faith and answered that ad in the paper.

Those years were interspersed with a year of decadence attending teacher's college across the pond in Glasgow, Scotland. I lived with five other Canadian students in an enormous apartment on Byres Road above a fishmonger. A pint of beer became one of my main food groups, and listening to live music in pubs was easily my favourite part of the year. (Shout-out to the talented and kind Big George—RIP). I met a few good friends there, dated a bit, and even went on my first solo vacation. Seeing the Queen drive right past me at the Highland Games (they really do toss those cabers, or tree trunks), looking for Nessie at Loch Ness, touring the Isle of Skye and Inverness, dancing at my first ceilidh, and visiting a multitude of castles all stand out in my hazy, alcohol-fueled memories. (In my defence, I'd just spent three years in a dry country.)

Mexico came after my second tour of academic duty in Kuwait. Aside from some light hiking in beautiful Chipinque, snake-skinning, being a newlywed, and hanging out with friends, holidaying on South Padre Island, visiting San Miguel de Allende (a gorgeous cobblestone city of artists), and driving north to meander along the San Antonio River Walk stand out in my memories.

After two years in Monterrey, Mike and I headed back to Canada to begin the next adventure of starting a family. So ended my years of international travel (a few gorgeous, all-inclusive resorts notwithstanding).

All these experiences built upon one another and added colour to my life. They changed the way that I thought, the way that I approached life, and the way that I saw the world. They changed who

I was. The fact that they mostly happened during my impressionable twenties added weight to them.

✳ ✳ ✳

Living life on the edge is not for the faint hearted. There are hidden dangers lurking beneath the rebellious waters. One afternoon in Kuwait, a group of us went on a trip to explore the desert. It was truly gorgeous with the rolling dunes and the golden-brown sand. My boyfriend and I wandered away from everyone and, *carpe diem* and all that, ended up ahem ... enjoying the moment. The dunes were high and we knew that no one would catch us *in flagrante delicto*. Later, we wandered back to the group secure in the knowledge that our stolen moments belonged to us and us alone.

Fast-forward a few weeks. We got invited to a poetry reading; my very first. I was taken aside preemptively by a lovely lady who kindly asked my permission to read her poem aloud.

Confusion must have showed on my face, so she continued to say that she had witnessed our "beautiful act" in the dunes and it had inspired her to put pen to paper.

Being fair-skinned and highly talented at blushing during inopportune moments, my skin was brick red. I tried to pull off the whole "European nonchalance about all things sexual" look (as much as a tomato can pull off that look), so I shrugged and replied, "Mais oui." I glided to the couch with a certain sangfroid, prepared to meet my fate.

Live life on the edge, take risks, and say yes to new experiences—just realize that one day you may find yourself immortalized in a poem.

Fair warning.

✳ ✳ ✳

Taking risks isn't always about travelling. One summer Saturday night I was out with friends Nance and Karla at a bar. It was packed to the brim and we, in our youthful miniskirted outfits, were having a blast. Pushing my way through the crowd en route to the washroom, I got stuck behind a large group of people. As I was patiently waiting for an opening in the masses, I overheard a guy and a girl talking over the cacophony. It went something like this:

Guy: "I grew up in Bora Bora. It was cool. So, I guess you could say that, yeah, I'm pretty well-travelled."

Girl: (insert Valley Girl intonation) "Oh. My Gawd. Like, No. Way. I can't believe I just met someone from Bora Bora."

Good Lord. Give me a break. What a line. Eyes

rolling, I tapped my foot as I waited. Was I going to be stuck listening to this scintillating conversation? I shot BS Guy and Vacuous Girl a withering stare but to no avail.

Suddenly, I was overtaken by an urge…

I turned to Guy, threw my arms open wide, and exclaimed, "It's you! I can't believe it! I haven't seen you since we were kids growing up in Bora Bora! How's your Aunt Betty?"

This could have gone very badly.

Instead, Guy hesitated a split second, and then spread his arms out wide too, replying, "It *is* you! It's been so long! Aunt Betty's great. How have you been? We've all missed you so much."

This was fun.

Girl (looking back and forth between us, eyes opened wide): "Oh. My. Gawd. You two grew up together in … Bora Bora and you haven't even seen each other since? And you just, like, bumped into each other in this bar? Like, *no* way."

After a few more minutes of fun, I excused myself and went along to the bathroom. When I came out, CF Guy (I had elevated him from BS Guy to Cute Funny Guy) was waiting for me. He put out his hand and said, "I have to meet you."

He was awesome, and yes, he was humourous, and yes, he was gorgeous. I had a boyfriend back in the States for the summer that I was being loyal to, though, so the adventure ended after a drink and a chat. Damned monogamy.

Sometimes being spontaneous and going outside your comfort zone really is fun.

Bora Bora is still on my travel list.

* * *

My mom is one fine looking lady—even at the ripe old age of eighty. She is, and has always been, gorgeous. When I was in high school, my friends used to say, "Have you *seen* Jackie's mom?"

Finishing a meal at a restaurant together shortly before Covid-19 rocked our world, I was walking with Mom to the car. I glanced at her, all dolled up and blurted, "Darn you, Mom—you are *still* smokin' hot!" Her head popped up from where she was busily fishing keys out of her purse and replied, "Smoke pot? Oh my. I've never done that but let's put it on my bucket list!"

Marijuana is legal now. I'm fairly pure in the drug department (wine notwithstanding). I have partaken in a smoke at an Amsterdam cafe (good place to try) and once in Kuwait (bad place to try) and ended up coughing my head off both times. It kind of ruins the vibe, not to mention that it's tricky to look nonchalant and cool when you're hacking up a lung. After my brief dabble into the dark world of the druggie, I let the whole "illegal substance thing" go by the wayside and carried on with life.

Until a beachside conversation one sunny afternoon involving talking my mom into trying some edibles (strike one thing off the ole bucket list), in hopes that some of her daily mounting anxiety would be abated.

Purchased drugs in hand from the aptly named "Stoner Station," a group of us gathered around the table, high-fiving each other. "Pot Party! Pot Party!" we chanted. We were wild and crazy all right. A bag of edible Skittles (they did look just like Skittles—this doesn't seem very wise, marketing managers, just saying) and chocolate graced our table, the music was rocking, conversation was flowing; we were in the zone.

Mom went home. Her bucket list would remain long.

The paper bag came out and the "Skittles" got handed around the group. One by one, we all passed for various reasons (driving later, early start for work in the morning, et cetera). Doug, rocking out to the music, and chatting up a storm, tossed down his "Skittle." Then, with an exuberant arm-raising fist pump and a final, "Pot Party!" chant, he realized that everyone was looking at him.

Just … him.

I haven't laughed that hard in a long time—and I was sober. I took much joy in asking him throughout the night how many fingers I was holding up or if I could get him some snacks.

We might never live down the story of our foray into the wild world of narcotics.

I did end up trying my colourful candy the next night. It was rather anticlimactic, apart from seeing Dumbo briefly (I would have preferred a naked Thor, but beggars can't be choosers). I'll try the chocolate next.

But Doug can go first.

Thank you, Mom, for the innocuous comment that led your children on a madcap adventure down a pharmaceutical rabbit hole.

✳ ✳ ✳

I'm tough as nails. I have a do-rag (okay-it's pink) for the motorcycle, a leather biker jacket, and black boots. Nobody messes with me as I glide down the street, giving the queen's wave to all I deign worthy while holding onto Dave for dear life. I'm also—as befitting any motorcycle mama worth her salt—all tatted up.

Yup. Four inked images desecrate my body.

Newly divorced, I decided that tattoos were befitting the next phase of my life. A family reunion and a halter-neck top afforded me the first oppor-tunity to present my works of art to the world. After a few days of body art boasting, I proudly strolled into the gathering and readied myself for the crowd's oohs and aahs. My aunt came to inspect first. Her tattooed sons and nephews have left her well-acquainted with the world of ink. She looked. She squinted. She went to get her glasses. She came back and looked again. She professed them the most petite tattoos she'd ever seen. My brother looked too.

"Jackie, I think you have four moles on your back—you should really get them looked at." My other siblings suggested that I had some dirt on me—did I want a cloth?

So maybe I'm not ready to join the Hell's Angels.

My tiny little birds soaring across my back shoul-der may not scream "Biker B*tch" to the world, but they do have a lot of meaning for me. Hours spent researching images led me to the poem "She Let Go" by Safire Rose. The version I found had a flock of birds imprinted across the page. Both the words and visuals resonated with where I was in my life; the decision was made.

The tattoo artist kept trying to convince me that I needed to upgrade in size given that the images were going on my back rather than, say, a wrist. Elegance and edginess could coexist, I countered.

Let my body be the canvas to demonstrate this to the world.

Hard-bitten, steely-yet-dainty Jackie. Henceforth please refer to me as The Tattoo Queen when you see me roar by.

I've got the wave down.

✳ ✳ ✳

I have a vague childhood memory of singing a church hymn that contained the lyrics, "*Knock and the door shall be opened unto you.*" Apparently I took those words to heart. Throughout my life I've literally knocked on three doors and ... lo and behold ... they all opened unto me.

The first was opened by a gentleman whose house on the lake Mike and I liked and thought had flipping potential. He sold. We bought. We renovated. We sold. My one and only experience as a land baron.

The second was opened by a retired couple who lived together in a five-bedroom home that was on the dream street, had the dream rec room, and the dream covered back porch. Dave and I thought that it would be perfect neutral turf on which to begin our blended family. They sold. We bought. We moved. We're still here. It's dreamy.

The last was opened by a family who owned my childhood home (where we had spent twenty-eight years). I was driving my mom around our old town for a trip down memory lane and decided to ask if they would consider letting us come back later for a tour. They pondered. They agreed. We laughed. We cried. We shared photos and told stories and it ended up sparking a lot of memories for us both—especially my mom.

Neither of the first two houses were up for sale. The people living in our old house were strangers. We just took a gamble. Sometimes putting yourself out there reaps rewards. And really, what have you got to lose?

"Ask and it shall be given unto you.
Seek and ye shall find."

LIFE LESSON #5

SUCK ALL THE MARROW OUT OF LIFE THAT YOU CAN.

Evelyn in *The Best Exotic Marigold Hotel* says, "But it's also true that the person who risks nothing, does nothing, has nothing. All we know about the future is that it will be different. But perhaps what we fear is that it will be the same."

I love that movie. Maybe one day, Dave and I will find ourselves living in India in a run-down hotel having a whole new adventure. I don't know what life has in store for us, but I truly hope it includes some spur-of-the-moment decisions that take us out of our comfort zone. There's an electric feeling of aliveness that happens when you are doing something new. Routines are lovely and dependable, but novelties can be invigorating. A balance between the two sounds good to me.

One lovely couple that I met in Kuwait became our *in loco parentis*. They retired early and realized one day that they didn't want to spend their golden years watching the cats play. They packed up and worked/travelled around the world for twenty-five years. My brother-in-law Richard bicycled across

Canada. Dave races fast cars on tracks. A friend of mine took a leap and created a new life for herself as a working artist.

You don't have to go to a war-torn country for an adventure. Excitement can be in the small, Bora Bora moments. It can be meeting your partner naked with a bottle of wine in your hands after work, saying, "Hi, Handsome. How was your day?" or in the huge moments like when my niece decided to be true to herself and transition.

I hope that whatever your version of living life is, you suck the marrow out of it. Make the most of that headstone dash.

Say "yes."

CHAPTER SIX

JUDGE NOT LEST YE BE JUDGED

*O*h, it's so easy to judge. I have worn the wig and gown and lowered the gavel many a time. I'm not proud of this. As I age, I have made a conscious effort to try and judge less. I'm no Buddha on the mountain, but ... I try.

Judge Gen on *The Good Place* eating a burrito with a dash of envy sauce, and doling out decisions with two thumbs down and a raspberry is the epitome of a cool judge. But, alas, I'm not an omniscient, immortal ruler of The Afterlife. I'm more like Eleanor with a whole lot of Chiti thrown in for good measure.

We all do it. We judge each other's parenting skills, looks, fashion sense, marriages, sex lives, physical prowess, lawns, jobs, cooking, houses, and even improper usage of subject-verb agreement (forgive me).

Don't hate me because my ivory tower is the nicest one on the block.

✷ ✷ ✷

I consider myself a good mom. Not a perfect mom, not even a great one, but a good one. (Unless feeding my offspring—gasp—canned baby food, McDonald's chicken fingers, and occasionally dessert before dinner strips me of my self-proclaimed title). I have invested a great deal of time and energy connecting with my kids; they're amazing young adults now and were amazing young children. I learned early on, however, not to pat myself on the back too much when they were well-behaved and not to berate myself too harshly when they messed up.

This message was brought home to me when Molly was in grade one. Molly was a quiet-spoken, well-behaved, and high-achieving (first born!) child. While driving to school one day, we were chatting about a new girl she had befriended and she was telling me that they were teaching each other new things.

I casually asked what Anna had taught her, and Molly responded matter-of-factly: "shit." My hands clenched the steering wheel, and my jaw pulsated. That girl was the devil's spawn. What kind of six-year-old talks like that? It must be the parents—it's always the parents. What was next? Drinking behind the recycling bins at recess? It was a slippery slope, and I could see it all too clearly.

Deeply mired in my own angry musings, I almost missed Molly's next sentence. In her high, sing-songy voice, Molly continued, "So I taught her one of the words I know, Momma. I taught her: 'f*ck.'"

Helicopter moms should never throw boulders in glass houses.

✳ ✳ ✳

Teef started life as LaTifa – Little LaTifa, to be exact. I was not a cat girl. I had, in fact, begged my parents for a dog more times than I could count growing up. In grade five I even gave a presentation to my parents with the prices of dog food, leash, collar, and newspaper cutouts advertising "puppies for free"—to no avail. They kept claiming they would be the ones who ended up walking it (they would have) and were unmoved by my continued pleas.

Cats were aloof. Cats were small. Cats were boring. Cats were not man's best friend. I had no interest in cats.

Heading into school in Kuwait to prep one weekend, my friend Tessa and I saw a tiny kitten. It alone had survived when its family had been killed on the road. The taxi driver who showed her to us didn't think she would live long. For some unfathomable reason, I scooped that kitten up and took it back to my apartment. Its ears were bigger than its body, and my principal pronounced it a bat. I named her Latifa after a sweet little girl in my class, and she was mine.

My family would soon howl at the thought of Teef being described as sweet and tiny.

Latifa survived the first few nights and started to thrive. She grew. I realized that "she" was actually a "he" and Latifa became Teef. I taught him to fetch. He loved eating olives. He was mine.

Until ... he wasn't. Teacher's college beckoned and Teef became a resident of Walkerton, population now 4,60*1*. My parents were far from thrilled but reluctantly agreed. I had the summer to acclimatize my family to Teef (not the other way around) before it was time to head off again. Perhaps I should have spent more than a hot minute contemplating getting a cat that day in the taxi, as my nomadic lifestyle wasn't entirely conducive to pet ownership.

A visit to the vet clinic was the first port of call once I returned home. Teef, although cuddly with me (and soon, my mom) was indifferent at best to some and flat-out aggressive to most. He should have come with a t-shirt spouting: "Underestimate me. That'll be fun." You can take the cat out of the alley but not the alley out of the cat.

When it was Teef's turn at the clinic, the veterinarian came out and pronounced that she would take him and that I could wait in the hall. I started to protest, saying that he was a handful and that it might be better if I came in, too.

She snickered a little, rolled her eyes at the receptionist, and sang out, "Overprotective mommy here!" She turned back to me, smiled and said in a slow, carefully enunciated manner: "We find that mommies do better when they can let go and let their babies be cared for by the professionals."

Visions floated through my head: Dad wearing oven mitts to pick him up, window screens ripped up weekly, scars down my brother's arms, furniture shredded.

I smiled an appropriately f*cking condescending smile back and replied, enunciating slowly, "That's fine, then. Mommy will stay right here."

The door shut. I leaned back, folded my arms, closed my eyes, and grinned.

Cue sitcom music. I literally heard crashing, banging, hissing, and a scream within minutes. The door flew open, and the woman stood before me, eyeglasses askew (hand on heart), red-faced, and hair mussed. She spit out, "Your cat has knocked over my entire shelving unit! Get him out of here!"

A huge shelving unit was sideways on the floor, boxes and supplies littered everywhere, and Teef ... well, Teef was surveying his handiwork from a high perch atop another shelving unit in the corner.

Good boy.

I looked left. I looked right. Finally, I pointed to myself in confusion. "Are you sure that you want Mommy to join you?"

Revenge is a dish best served cold.

I doubt that the lovely veterinarian ever again judged a "mommy" as being too overprotective.

Teef lived a long life and became my mother's fifth and favourite child. He was even elevated to role model for my brother's friends. Teef had a habit of coming up to you, turning around, and tapping your foot with his back paw when he wanted food. David's friends started emulating him at the bars. Seeing a grown man turn around and tap my brother on the foot when hoping for a beer was freaking hilarious.

Turns out cats are pretty cool.

My stepchildren Madelynn and Braeden introduced us to the show *The Fosters* when we all moved in together in 2015. Had I been able to view the series back in 1990 it would have helped prepare me for the challenges to come.

Although Natalie was my foster child for only a short time, she and her mom taught me a lot about making assumptions. When you've had an easy life growing up within a loving, white, middle-class family, it's hard to remember that others didn't have the same starting line. Some weren't even on the same track.

I was angry at her mother for all the times Natalie had to get herself and her younger siblings up, dressed, and fed, and then make their way to school. I was angry that she had frostbite scars on her face. And I was angry that her mother told her I would be her foster mother before I was even asked. Opening my door one day to find Natalie on my doorstep was a shock, as was hearing her say that her mom was going away, her siblings were being fostered out, and that her mom told her she could come to live with me if I said yes.

Proper channels and paperwork filed, I dove into another new experience, with an equal mix of trepidation and excitement.

Natalie's body was covered with eczema – she was embarrassed to wear shorts and t-shirts in the summer. A couple of doctor's visits and tubes of cream later and she was proudly running around in a bathing suit. The fact that she had dealt with this easily solvable issue for so long irked me.

So ... yes ... I judged. In my mind (although I'd never met her), Natalie's mom had few redeeming qualities. I would swoop in and make all the difference. She was an intelligent girl, funny, resilient, and full of potential and I, why I would help her thrive.

We took her to my uncle's lakefront stone cottage for two weeks of boating, with a side of swimming lessons tossed in. Natalie loved the boat, and especially enjoyed gleeful sparring with quick-witted Uncle Johnny as we zipped across the lake. Swimming lessons—not so much. Watching me suntan on the front lawn lounge chair one day, Natalie asked me why some white people want to be dark and some dark people want to be white. "Can't they all just be happy with how they are?" Out of the mouths of babes.

My family and I showered her with gifts that summer: Barbies, books, baseball and bat, soccer ball, new clothes. We read together every night. Settled on the family room couch one night, Natalie stumbled over the word "patience." When I jumped in to help her, she told me with a mischievous smile that I just needed more "patience." At eight years of age, she was decidedly self-sufficient but revelled in one-on-one attention.

I was figuratively patting myself on my back for my young, new "mothering" skills. Look how healthy she was! How happy! What a difference I was making!

So ... when the mail started coming in, it was an eye-opener. Beautiful, hand-drawn cards came regularly for Natalie from her mom in rehab. She was a talented artist and wrote loving, humourous messages to Nat letting her know how well she was doing and how much she missed her. I started to view things from a different lens. Maybe she wasn't the devil incarnate. Maybe, she was just a woman trapped in a cycle from which it was hard to break free. Maybe she was just a woman struggling, like millions before her, with addictions. Maybe she was just a woman with four children under the age of eight that she was trying to raise on her own.

One Saturday I took Nat out for lunch at the local greasy spoon. Natalie, noticing two men sitting together eating, suddenly got up and went over to them.

"Do you know Brian?" she asked one of the men.

"Sure, I do. Brian's my friend."

"Well, Brian's my dad. Next time you see Brian tell him his daughter Natalie says hey." Nat, showing no expression, returned, sat down, and carried on eating as if nothing had happened. My heart broke a little that day.

When the time came to return Natalie, my parents and I drove her partway to meet her mom. They would travel further north together, heading home to meet up with her siblings and be a family again. After Natalie ran up and hugged her mom, they turned and walked away together, leaving a hockey bag filled with the new summer toys behind. Vivid yellow, blue, brown, and red bits poked out of the top. All the material things that we had lavished upon her were meaningless to Nat in the end. She was with her mom again, who was healthy, and that was what mattered.

One of my all-time favourite characters in one of my all-time favourite books, Atticus Finch in *To Kill a Mockingbird*, said:

"You never really understand a person until you consider things from his point of view - until you climb into his skin and walk around in it."

Exactly right, Atticus. Exactly right.

✷ ✷ ✷

Making an appearance at a party one year with mainly young Kuwaitis in attendance was an education. My eyes flitted around the crowd and settled on the women sitting scattered throughout the living area in their dark abayas. With an inward sigh I thought, "Well, this party is going to be wild and crazy," as I mentally prepared myself for a rousing game of Trivial Pursuit. Those young women suddenly stood up and took off their coverings and—lo and behold—were dressed in vibrant and scanty attire. That party really was wild and crazy and those women put my dance moves to shame.

This was the beginning of my paradigm shift.

I felt inordinately sorry for the Kuwaiti women for a while. Their lives seemed sad. Few worked, many wore the dark abayas in the relentless heat, arranged marriages were common, and men reigned supreme. Although much freer than women in other Muslim countries, their lives were shrouded in restrictions, at least according to Judging Jackie.

So, it was a shock to me when, after eating lunch and swimming at the pool of a Kuwaiti woman and mother of a student, she shared that the Kuwaiti women pitied ... me. From their viewpoint, Western women lived an empty existence, devoid of real meaning. Kuwaitis lived with their extended family and houses were always filled with children and elders. The concept of living alone or of putting your parents in an "old-age home" was entirely foreign to them. Family was everything. They felt that

Western women were stretched too thin between raising our children without help and climbing the corporate ladder. They believed that we were always searching for the perfect romance when we should just make the most of who we were matched with.

Kuwait is a ridiculously wealthy nation, and the "first-tier" families were extraordinarily well off. The women shopped with a Prada fervour and bought gold jewelry like it was going extinct. In their eyes, we led lives of discontent, always working, always searching, and perpetually lonely and unhappy. They were surrounded by family, lived a life of luxury, and travelled often. Who pitied whom?

I believe what this woman shared was true. It's probably also true that life was easier on Western women in the 1950s when gender roles were relatively set in stone. However, it came with the caveat that you were white, safe in your relationship, and content to be a homemaker. If you weren't, then life probably sucked. I feel the same about the Kuwaiti women. If you were in an unhappy situation, then your options were few. I'll bet more than a few women have wished that the words, "I divorce thee, I divorce thee, I divorce thee" held the same power for them as when uttered by men.

Overall, though, what I took from this was that there are happy and unhappy people everywhere.

Watching children playing soccer with a deflated ball in Thailand, no shoes, ragged clothes, yet laughing and smiling, was uplifting. Nicaragua is one of the poorer countries and yet has a remarkably low suicide rate. Making assumptions about the happiness of others based on their cultural norms or even their wealth (or lack thereof) was a mistake.

Glass houses come in all shapes and sizes.

Visiting Bethlehem on Christmas Eve, the year Palestine got control, was exciting. It was 1995, and the Palestinian police had arrived to take control of the city on December 21. Soldiers dressed in body armour, holding their automatic rifles, had stood by for the handover of power. I'd been very excited about the visit. The anticipation of being at the Church of the Nativity was the segment of my vacation that I most looked forward to. I was then—and still remain—a hopeful agnostic. Still, Christmas Eve has always been the most inherently meaningful religious date for me. I couldn't wait to be there. However, instead of a profoundly reverent moment in time, I experienced genuine fear. Palestinian leader Yasser Arafat delivered a speech from the church's roof that night—above the place traditionally held to be the site of Jesus' birth. Thousands of Palestinians chanted, yelled—fists pumping in the air—danced, and sang loudly. Pushing and shoving in excitement, throngs of men were literally everywhere, jostling us in their celebration. Although a choir was singing, I couldn't hear a word. Without much thought given to the history and meaning that led to that moment, all I felt was irritation. How dare they ruin *my* magical Christmas Eve? The nerve.

Make some room at the inn, people.

I don't profess to know who is right or wrong in the Palestinian/Israeli conflict. I'm lacking a whole lot of knowledge and wisdom. These days I try to confine my judgements to a person's actions rather than their motivation. It's impossible to truly know someone else's motivation with any degree of accuracy. Yes, the masses were unruly, but they were also joyful and I don't suspect that their intent was to ruin my Christmas Eve. Their version of a wondrous December 24 was every bit as valid as mine that night.

I ended up spending Christmas Eve eating at a diner with friends and, although no angels did we hear on high, we were safe, together, and happy.

Maybe that's what it's all about after all.

✳ ✳ ✳

If it looks like a duck, swims like a duck, and quacks like a duck, it might be a chicken. Or a robin. Or even a hedgehog.

I'm an equal mix of gregarious and shy—the waxing and waning of the moon perhaps determine which rises to the forefront at any given moment. One year, new to a school in Ottawa, I decided it was time to get to know some of my coworkers. I made up little "Chick-Flick" flyers and stuffed them into mailboxes, inviting several women to come over one evening for wine, cheese and crackers, and some Matthew McConaughey on the side. To my delight, all said yes, and I readied my home for the occasion. I really do hate the drop-in visit but love planned entertaining. I can at least pretend to be organized, clean, and tidy. By the time I open my door for guests, even Marie Kondo herself would feel at peace. God knows when fresh bathroom hand towels would come out if I wasn't hosting.

As the evening progressed and more wine (aka truth serum) was consumed, we started sharing and confiding in each other. One of the ladies turned to me and said, "You're nothing like I thought you were. I totally had you pegged as a bit snooty."

The others started laughing and agreed. "I called you Lady Di in my head!"

"Right? She glides by me sometimes and doesn't even acknowledge me."

"And her perfect tan!"

I was utterly flabbergasted. Me? Snooty? And then I started laughing, holding my stomach and laughing till it hurt. (Thank you, Kegels.) When I finally contained myself, I explained that I had taken ballet in my childhood and always had the stern voice of my teacher in my head:

"Jacqueline, pretend you are carrying a book on your head at all times. Shoulders down. Chin up. Stomach in."

I continued to explain that I am perhaps slightly vain and nearsighted. I need glasses to drive, watch TV clearly, and see anyone distinctly that's not reasonably close to me. Conversely, I don't need glasses to see up close and am happily without cheaters while I read. I've tried bifocals, but they just make me dizzy. To make out the actual facial figures of people from afar, I have to squint and look closely, which can appear rather disconcerting. So I compromise and give a vaguely polite, microscopic smile to anyone within my general vicinity. Damned vanity.

And my perfect tan? I had tried a spray tan to ready myself for a wedding, one at which I would be seeing friends (aka an old boyfriend) that I hadn't seen for many years. I was going for a last-minute

Hail Mary. I was new to the whole spraying world. My hairdresser had suggested it as they offered the service at the salon. I casually asked what you wear during said adventure and was told to bare it all.

Okay. Well, yes, I've skinny-dipped, and yes, I've European spa-ed. I could do this.

This wasn't a lie-in-a-tanning-bed experience or standing in a shower. Mais no. This was an actual person spritzing me with a handheld dealio. I took a deep breath and flung open the curtain.

Shoulders down. Chin up. Stomach in.

I could handle the face, neck, and chest area. The abdomen was acceptable, too. As the poor girl knelt lower, I struggled to make small talk (kind of like while getting a Pap smear). How 'bout those Jays? God love her, she barely flinched and stoically continued with her art. At the end of the experience, she casually mentioned that perhaps I might like to use the paper thong that had been tastefully provided in the change room next time. Thong? Not a tissue? It had been so very useful while blotting nervous sweat.

I made some new friends that night. Sometimes a little background knowledge changes our perspectives entirely.

∗ ∗ ∗

Molly had a large group of friends in grade ten, and, on a warm sunny day, they would meander over to the nearby park at lunchtime. They were a mix of boys and girls: still kids on the inside, yet in the dreaded high-school years of jockeying for position and a sense of belonging. Trying to fit in and be cool while still being true to yourself is the bane of every young teenager's existence. Levels of party-going separated the students into cliques. I was pretty sure I knew which level they were at, but hey, what do the parents really know?

After about twenty minutes of hanging at the park, a formidable-looking police officer drove up, exited his vehicle, and strode towards them.

Feet apart, arms behind his back, he stared down the ashen-faced, wide-eyed youths. Silence ensued.

Finally, in a terse, gruff voice, he barked out, "We've had a complaint from one of the neighbours. She reported that you lot are drinking, doing drugs, and are generally being loud and disruptive to the community."

Frozen in fear, the kids stayed silent.

"I've been watching you though and see ... that you are playing grounders. Carry on."

The kids probably would have gotten a lot of street cred at school if they had been "busted" for breaking the law at lunch. The story remained a tightly sealed secret. Crazy shenanigans such as cavorting and playing tag on the monkey bars just didn't quite cut it as rebellious behaviour.

Kids these days.

LIFE LESSON #6

GET DOWN OFF THAT HIGH HORSE AND BE A LITTLE BIT KINDER.

We're all Judgey McJudgers sometimes. Try going a day without mentally judging someone; I dare you.

I have clutched my pearls many a time. I admit to judging other parents on their rules for their children, especially regarding boundaries, under-age drinking, amount of partying, et cetera. Over the years, I've watched these kids grow up. Some of those kids who had more freedom to experiment turned out to be kind, responsible, and productive individuals. Some who had tighter controls struggled later in life. Vice versa, too. I think it just boils down to the connection that you have with your kids rather than what rules you choose to impose. With a strong connection, kids will generally turn to you when they need to. Maybe some of it is luck, too.

Why did I judge? Fear? Probably. Prop myself up and put others down to feel better about myself? Likely. Pat myself on the back for the parenting mistakes I would never make? I'm sure.

One of my adult friends scared me to death while we were in high school. She was brilliant, athletic, and artistic and strode through the school with a sense of purpose and confidence. She was tough and cool while I ... at least in my own head ... was not. We became close friends in later years, and when I told her that she intimidated the crap out of me at that time, she howled. It turns out she was lonely and hated her high school years with a passion. She ate lunch in the art room to avoid the whole cafeteria "with whom do I sit" scenario.

No one has it made. We just all make judgments about ourselves and others and then take them as the gospel truth without questioning whether or not our lens is foggy.

Gary Zukhov, the author of *The Seat of the Soul*, says that: "At the heart of judging other people is the feeling of being unworthy—less than, inferior."

Instead of accepting your emotions, it's easier to judge and/or lash out, to try to change the other person and make yourself look or feel better. When you figure out what's making you feel insecure, you might as well try to deal with it because otherwise, it'll just keep coming back to bite you.

Another strategy is to put yourself in the other person's position. When you start to see things through different eyes, your perceptions change. Apparently, Atticus Finch was right all along. It's just tough to do—especially in the moment.

Victor Frankl said that: "Between stimulus and response there is a space. In that space is our power to choose our responses. In our response lies our growth and our freedom."

I had this quote hanging in my grade seven classroom, as much as a reminder to myself as to the students. If we can catch ourselves when we're judging others and pause, maybe, with a lot of practice, we can learn to choose a kinder, more compassionate response.

As my guy Ted Lasso says (via Walt Whitman): Be curious, not judgmental. Perhaps that's the very best strategy of all.

CHAPTER SEVEN

NINE TO FIVE

My son Finn went through an *Office* craze and when Finn gets in a phase, step aside, watch and learn. Rubik's cubing, basketball, writing rap lyrics, producing music, school, working out—he puts his full concentration and focus on whatever he's doing, and becomes an expert. No lack of follow through for this kid. (In this respect, both he and Molly take after their father.) This carries over to viewing pleasure. When he's on a roll with a show, he's really on a roll. *The Office* was one that I was happily on board with.

One day he had me do a "Which TV Character Are You Most Like" quiz—clearly a solid use of

Covid-19 time. Pam Beasley was my top match. What made me laugh, though, was the fact that Pam Beasley was given the birthday of March 25, my birthday (and Kyle Lowry's too—good company we keep). I was Pam! Pam, I am!

Pam made the most of her job. Being a receptionist in a paper company might not have been the most exciting career in the world, but she found ways to make it home. Falling in love with her coworker probably didn't hurt.

Over the years I have worked in a multitude of roles. Some were physically difficult, some were fun, and some were intellectually stimulating, but every one taught me something, even if it was just to stay in school.

★ ★ ★

As a closet *People* magazine reader with a secret yen for acting, I have always imagined that I would eventually make the acquaintance of celebrities. I would be cool, impervious to celebrity pandering. No desperate plea for an autograph or coquettish selfie request from me. No, I would casually and politely toss off something like, "I admire your work, Brad," or "Hi Matt, I enjoyed the Bourne series," as I threw them a wave and continued on my Rodeo Drive shopping spree. Maybe I would bump into Jen and make a witty, self-deprecating comment as we both reached for the same size zero (ha!) black strapless dress. She would crack up, and conversation would flow—instant friends. Or maybe I'd be wandering around Lake Como, and George and I would strike up a conversation about tequila (I can only add insightful opinions about Diet Coke, but I would fake it). Several hours later, Amal and I would be deep into discussions about the Middle Eastern conflict and international human rights.

Alas, nary a celebrity has crossed my path.

Finn and Molly met Wayne Gretzky's dad Walter while out hiking one day. My stepdad ate his lunch beside Eric Clapton in Japan. I saw Kyle Lowry at my son's basketball camp. Goldie and Kurt had a cottage a few hours away from me for a while. And Madelynn has a life-sized cardboard Harry Styles somewhere in the basement.

That's it. That's the culmination of my brush with the rich and famous. No rubbing elbows. Not even a six-degrees-of-Kevin-Bacon situation.

There was however, one night when I had the opportunity to meet a band—a quasi-well-known Canadian band. Surely that counts.

An inn was the site of my brief career as a front-desk clerk. The hotel wasn't large enough to make the job stressful but was just big enough to make it fun. This was pre-computer check-in days, so every reservation that I took went into a huge book in pencil. The writing was on the wall regarding my soon-to-be teaching career as I got an immense satisfaction out of printing neatly with a new, freshly sharpened pencil. Even carefully erasing cancelled reservations brought me joy. It's a sickness, I know.

Answering the phone, helping with daily requests, and meeting new people made the job interesting and different every day. Greeting the guests was often entertaining. I'll never forget the family from the US who were bitterly disappointed to find a snowless summer in Guelph as they drove in with their skis on the car rack. Look on map, people.

It was a couple of weeks before Halloween when I met them: a group of amiable guys checking in and hanging around my desk to chat. They told me that they were "The Grapes of Wrath." It seemed a little early to be heading to a Halloween party but hey, go for it. They tried in vain to explain to me that they were not, in fact, going to a party wearing green balloons with angry faces drawn on them. That they were a legitimate band and Grapes of Wrath was their name. They sang a few lines from their top songs. Nothing. They harmonized. Nada. They told me the names of their albums. Zero.

I tried to cheer them up. I pretended that at least

a couple of songs sounded familiar. But hey, I was just one lowly little front-desk clerk, so who cares? When I passed this story on to my guy friends the next day, they were aghast at my general lack of truly excellent musical knowledge.

I'm sorry, Grapes of Wrath. You deserved better. I'm sure that the staff at your next hotel were much more musically informed. Thank you for being my first brush with fame. I admire your work.

The inn is no longer but my time there won't soon be forgotten. That role gave me the opportunity to interact with a multitude of people and gain experience in dealing with a wide range of personalities in various states of happiness. Calming down irate guests was an art form that I strove to perfect and that skill served me well in my future career. It also spawned in me a lifelong habit of tidying up hotel rooms before checking out.

The Ewings are an honest bunch. Doug wins the highly coveted "Most Honest Golfer" award each summer. Lisa is meticulous in following the rules in her career as a chartered accountant. And David, well, David would only tell a lie when, after waiting in line three hours to get a ticket to his favourite band, he would say, "That's okay, I've seen them before—you take the last spot" to the despondent-looking guy behind him. And me? I still feel pangs of conscience over taking credit for a painting that I didn't do in grade four.

It was a painting of Peter Pan. The girl who created it didn't want it, so I took it home. My parents, thinking I was an artistic genius, hung it on the wall and proudly showed it off to all and sundry who entered our hallowed home. I've never been able to watch *Hook* without developing an eye tic. The shame eats away at my black soul. I should probably be Catholic but sadly, I'm the worst kind of Protestant: all the guilt with none of the work ethic. Since this "come to Jesus" moment however, I have generally tried to stick to the straight and narrow.

But ... the empty "clink" when dropping a coin into my piggy bank meant that desperate times required desperate measures. A few blocks away from my house in university was a restaurant advertising for an experienced server. I could walk there in minutes. I would have cash-on-hand tip money plus a biweekly check. The only thing holding me back was my utter lack of food-serving experience. I squared my shoulders and prepared to prevaricate. Dissemble. Tell untruths even, pushing the fact that I blush like a Royal Gala to the back of my head.

Bessie and Chris were the owners and the talent at the diner. Short, stout, cheerful, hair-netted Bessie was the cook in the steaming hot kitchen and, equally short, marginally less stout, and infrequently cheerful Chris, her husband, held court in a table by the front of the restaurant, incessantly chatting with men at his booth, going over numbers, and drinking cup after cup of coffee. The greasy aroma made my stomach growl. Fries and gravy were calling my hips.

The interview was brief.

Did I have experience. Um … sure. Yeah. I worked part-time at our local diner in my hometown, for over a year. Sure, I could hit the ground running. No, I wasn't feeling hot or sick. No, I didn't need air. Why do you ask?

I was hired.

My first shift came the following weekend. The real server was busily moving about, cleaning tables, restocking napkin holders, and refilling the coffee pot when I got there. I shadowed her for about an hour and was starting to feel quite comfortable. There were only three occupied tables—two with single, elderly men and one with two elderly women. Mostly they wanted a cup of coffee or tea and a sandwich. I could do this.

Abruptly, Real Waitress announced that her shift was over. Since I was so experienced, Bessie and

Chris figured I could handle the evening crowd on my own. I believe she smirked a little as she repeated this to me—having borne witness to my novice actions. How do you turn on a pot of coffee? Filters? As a tea girl, hailing from a long line of tea drinkers, making coffee was like learning Mandarin.

Fifteen minutes passed. Then another ten. Just one more little old lady came in. Tea and a grilled cheese sandwich with fries. I started walking more confidently. "*It Could Happen to You*" hadn't come out yet, but if it had, I would surely have been imagining myself splitting a lottery ticket with a handsome police officer soon. I hummed along to the radio as I importantly straightened forks and lined up knives and spoons.

A burst of laughter at the front door made me look up. Two men entered the building wearing baseball uniforms, talking animatedly, followed by a host of further male testosterone. Fifteen, I counted. Fifteen laughing, sweaty, starving customers. Fifteen. Before I could say a silent "God help me" under my breath, the door opened again and a family of five wandered in.

I earned my money that night. Luckily the men were friendly and went easy on me. A lot of jokes, a few pitchers of beers, some minor (okay, major) flirting, and they were patient with my many order mix-ups. The family of five ... not so much.

At the end of the night Bessie looked at me and said, "You've never waitressed before, Jackie, have you? That's okay. We like you. We'll keep you."

They liked me. They kept me.

Years later my father continued to bemoan my server job. Forevermore, when eating out with my mom, Mom would whisper, "Remember Jackie!" when it was time to leave a tip. Double the going tipping percentage rate was the only thing that would assuage her.

He would also lament my brief stint as a telemarketer. "Remember Jackie," Mom would hiss as he was about to hang up when asked about buying a one-year subscription to *National Geographic*. Resigned to his fate, Dad would suffer in silence to the monologue as the magazines piled up. I'm sure he wished I had sold hockey cards. (His collection was impressive—even though his child had signed her name on all of his best cards. Forgive me, Dad. I'm sure I felt that a barely legible "JACKIE" would add to their worth one day.)

I developed a newfound respect for waitstaff while working at the restaurant. Sore feet, rude customers, minimum wage, and plastering a perpetual smile on your face through it all is far from easy. I did learn how to think on my feet (literally), how to multitask, and continued to develop my de-escalation skills. I empathize with waitstaff everywhere now and submit that everyone should do a service role of some kind over the course of a lifetime. Walk a mile.

Finn has taken up the mantle in the Honest Ewing club. I tried to prep him for his first-ever job interview at a pharmacy, warning him that he would probably get asked about his strengths and weaknesses. I recommended that he find a way to turn a weakness into a strength, such as, "I've never worked a cash register before, but I learn new things quickly."

They asked the question and Finn responded with, "My people skills aren't the best, my confidence needs work, and I talk way too fast." Out of six students, they hired Finn because ... they admired his honesty.

No Peter Pan tic issue for that boy.

✳ ✳ ✳

I've always been a tad mercurial and a little prone to rumination and envy. Not overly mind you, but probably more than the average bear. On the Big Five Personality Test, I score about a 56 in neuroticism. (But really, how accurate are these things are when we score ourselves? Maybe I'm an oblivious 90.) So, when I encounter people in life who are naturally contented with their lot, I look at them in awe and ask what their parents did when they were young. Breast or bottle? Mozart or Morrison? Nurture or nature? Spare or spoil?

I used to think that you could only be happy at work if you were in the perfect job. It made sense. If you like what you're doing for at least forty hours a week, then you're going to be cheerful. This theory pans out to a degree —I don't think that life as a ski instructor would be my nirvana. However, I also think there is a healthy dose of "it is what you make it" thrown into the mix.

Picture a stifling hot factory, filled with people completing one simple action, minute after minute, hour after hour, day after day, month after month, and year after year. My role, when I worked as a pants folder, was to take pants off the conveyor belt, fold them, and put them on the next rack. (I got tendinitis after a month of this.)

I will never forget the glut of Italian women who surrounded me in the factory.

They would sing. Every single day.

Laughing, chatting, but mostly singing, they would complete their eight hours before going home to whatever life held for them there. Make supper? Stop for groceries? Pick up the kids? Drink wine and read a book in the comfort of a pristine one-bedroom apartment? While away the hours making love to a twenty-years-younger stallion?

I'll never know, but I remain filled with reverence at their ability to turn a mind-numbing job into a place of community and happiness. I'm not saying that they went around in a state of constant bliss but ... wow. I can get derailed by an indoor recess, so hats off to them.

Sanding furniture one summer in a factory also brought this lesson home. There was no singing to be heard but some of the guys had me flat out laughing every day. Totally covered in dust, clocking in and out like Fred Flintstone, and doing manual work on different types of wood each day would have been a nightmare for me if not for the company. I don't know if I've ever laughed that much at a job since.

Rock picking, strawberry planting, haying (does four hours count?), scooping ice cream, house cleaning, photocopying (yup) ... I've done a lot of manual jobs. I take my hat off to all those people who can do them every day.

Then there are those who take enormous pride in their work and it shows.

I turned thirty while on vacation in Switzerland. I was heading up to Interlaken and was rushing to catch a train. With my cumbersome backpack swaying mightily behind me, I huffed and puffed to make it to the platform on time. I wanted to catch the 8:00 a.m. train and had slept in, not being a particularly early riser. In my memories I was like a contestant on *The Amazing Race*, breathlessly racing to the next transportation point.

I ran to the ticket counter where a lone, meticulously dressed, middle aged man sat, straight-backed in his seat. Leaning against the booth I managed to say, between pants, "Has the eight o'clock train left yet?"

Twenty-five years later, the look of disdain that briefly flashed across his face still cracks me up.

"Ja. It's 8:02," he replied curtly.

Like, of course, you idiot. Do you dare to insinuate that MY TRAIN, on MY PLATFORM, at MY STATION would leave at anything other than the exact time it was due to leave? Imbecile. Cretin. Boor.

If you want to buy something that works well and will work for a long time, buy Swiss. Pride in a job well done. Even the homes and properties were scrupulously maintained.

I will never again question a Swiss ticket master.

I may have two degrees, come from a white, middle-class home and a loving family background, but I missed the memo at birth saying to make the most out of whatever job you're doing—to be content. It really is a choice. Thank you to all the people who showed me that it is possible.

***

My career as a pinup girl was brief, yet illustrious. On a scorching hot afternoon at the beach in Kuwait, my friends and I met a group of young American men. They started nudging each other, whispering "It's her!" barely concealed behind covered hands.

It was her. Me. Famous. Apparently, exiting the water one afternoon, a photo of me was taken on the sly only to be blown up and hung on an apartment wall.

I know, I know. Creepy, distasteful, and objectifying. I agree. There was a small piece of me—deeply buried in lifelong insecurities—that felt flattered that my twenty-five-year-old self was blowup worthy. Until I remembered that I was a female in a Muslim, post-war, currently sparsely populated country, in a bathing suit, on a beach littered with Scud missiles.

My modeling career began and ended quickly. No royalties passed hands. I'll get an agent next time the paparazzi come calling.

***

My two uncles were teachers. Four of my aunts were teachers. My dad was a teacher. My mom was a teacher. I was never, ever, going to be a teacher. My afternoons were not spent lining up stuffed animals in rows as "students." Nope, I "sold" tickets to plays in our grandparents' basement.

Looking back, however, a clear path seems evident, although I fought it every inch of the way. I spent several summers babysitting five days a week, became a live-in nanny to the most amazing family, and tutored special-needs students. I loved kids. I've always felt immediately comfortable in the presence of children and teens, far more so than with most adults. I still do.

In my third and fourth year at university, I started to realize that my Honours English degree might pose a challenge in terms of finding a job. Editor? Maybe. Journalism? Not cutthroat enough for that. Law school? I can't even wear a blazer without feeling like I'm suffocating.

Everyone kept suggesting teaching and I negated the idea with an impatient flick of my hand.

Finally, one day I decided to go to a nearby school and see if I could volunteer. Standing in the hall and looking at a bulletin board, I knew. I knew that this was where I belonged. That utter feeling of rightness. Our kids have all toured university campuses before choosing their school and they all say that they "got the feel" when they walked through the right one. I "got the feel" that day and

I never looked back.

Unscheduled train rides and Freudian slip parties were fun, but keeping my grades up hadn't made the top of my priority list. (Delayed gratification and Jackie don't always see eye to eye. I would definitely have eaten the marshmallow.) And filling in piles of paperwork was about as appealing to me as a root canal. So I didn't even bother to apply to teacher's college when I was getting ready to graduate. Instead I took a more circuitous route which, although exciting, was probably a little more stressful.

I have loved teaching most of the time and liked it the rest of the time. I get to use some of my dramatic flair while presenting lessons, can throw in a bit of singing here and there, and get to connect with kids all day long. The kids make all the difference. I genuinely like and care deeply about every student I teach—even if it takes a bit of patience, humour, and initiating games at recess to find some way to make a connection. Every year I call them "my" kids. They'll always be my kids.

I have a lot of kids.

Looking back, I can see that my front-desk job helped me learn to de-escalate rising tempers, my server job got me used to being on my feet all day and multitasking, my photocopying gig—well that came in handy— and my manual jobs made me realize how much I need to be emotionally invested in what I do. I also take pride in my job. Thank you, Mister Train Ticket Master guru.

Teaching isn't the only job I would have loved. Being a counsellor would have been a good fit. Doing something creative and media-related would have also been a perfect match. Maybe even acting. Over the years I have joked repeatedly about starting a phone-sex business: just me, some comfy pjs, a bag of Ruffles, and a chance to try out a wide variety of accents. A few mumbled, "Oh baby, oh baby, oh babies" interspersed with chomping potato chips as I kept half an eye on the latest *General Hospital* episode seemed to be a sound business plan. Really, how tough could it be? Lisa rightly points out, however, that given our techie age, live video calls might be required now. I was born in the wrong age. My friend Anita wants in on the company. We've decided to name it: Anita-Jac-Off Inc. Look for us on billboards everywhere.

I look forward to seeing where our four kids' aptitudes, focus, and drive take them. They will all be well-prepared to put Dave and me into high-quality (i.e., expensive) nursing homes one day, but more importantly, I feel confident that they will find a work/life balance that makes them happy. I put about two percent thought into this stuff when I was their age, so kudos to them. Many of the jobs my peers do now didn't exist when we were in university, so I also hope they stay open to veering off the chosen path. As a caveat, however, I want them to remember that *any* job, no matter how much you like it, is going to come with some boring, stressful, and downright crappy days, the occasional irritating coworker, and more hours than you might like. That's just the way it is. You don't like that? We have a room in the basement. A little bit of struggle and discomfort in life is a healthy thing. Dip your toe in a variety of environments and see if you get "the feel." If not, figure out what you can take away from the role—because you will gain skills everywhere you go—even if it's just learning to interact with different personalities.

LIFE LESSON #7

BET ON YOURSELF.

Over the course of my many work-lives, I've learned one crucial lesson: I can count on myself. I learned that, when needed, I can find a way to support myself. I wasn't too proud to take whatever I could find and I learned that I could adapt to a wide variety of situations, even ones I wasn't very good at. (You probably shouldn't tend bar without at least knowing how to pour a beer without a head on it.) I picked up a lot of different skills and, in the end, learned that it was important for me to follow one of my passions in life—even if it took me a while to figure out what that was.

We could all find multiple careers that would bring us happiness. It's unlikely that one job is going to make you happy all the time.

If you want to do something unorthodox, a tad unrealistic and maybe not a good money bet, give yourself five years and just go for it. Do it before you get mired with mortgages and commitments that put "following your passion" lower on the priority list. What have you got to lose? If you're going to spend thirty-plus years doing something, it might as well be something that you genuinely like if not love. The younger generation is way better at this than we were.

Maybe you'll bet on yourself later in life and finally sit down and put some words on a blank piece of paper. Changing course is totally feasible and can be invigorating. Break free of those golden handcuffs if they're too tight. Great salaries and pensions plus children and mortgages make it difficult to take a leap. But kids will grow up, mortgage payments will end and ... there's still time.

My mom bet on herself. She didn't go to university after high school, following the path of least resistance for women at the time and became a secretary. Mom always regretted that decision and later decided to do something about it as she was approaching middle age. She started going to night school and taking distance courses (online would have made her life much easier) while working as a town librarian and raising four children. Her perseverance paid off, and she graduated from university and then proceeded to get her Masters of Library Science, followed by her Bachelor of Education at Toronto. This required her to live in the city, so she rode a bus three hours every Monday morning and Thursday night to accommodate that requirement. In the end, she was hired at our town high school, where she worked as a librarian until she retired.

She went after what she wanted, even though it wasn't easy, and it took her years. That's determination. That's impressive. That's my mom.

My alter ego Pam advised, "Just go after what you want and act fast, because life just isn't that long."

Bet on yourself. Figure out what brings you joy and find a way to get paid doing it. And, along the way, pick up new skills, make the most out of your jobs, and take pride in whatever it is that you're doing.

CHAPTER EIGHT

CHIN UP

When June became Offred in *The Handmaid's Tale*, her daily existence became a nightmarish mix of subjugation, subservience, rape, and physical abuse. In short ... hell. I don't live in Gilead, and my life has been comparatively benign thus far. Here's the thing, though: if life hasn't kicked you in your figurative abdomen yet, leaving you gasping for breath at least once or twice, just wait—it will. We don't get through this world without a least a little of that. Sometimes it sneaks up on you, and sometimes you get fair warning of the approaching earthquake, but either way, once you've navigated the pain, you're left with two choices: get up or stay down. That's it. Unless you want to live life as a husk of a shell, you're going to have to get up eventually. Figuring out how to do that and then actually doing it, now that's the tricky part.

✴ ✴ ✴

My grandmother is ninety-eight and a half (half years count when you get to her age) and is still going strong. She lives in an apartment building in her two-bedroom unit on the second floor (sans elevator). The laundry is in the basement. She has been bleaching the doorknobs and handrails in the building since she moved in and has never met a hotel room that hasn't loved Javex. The woman was born ready for this pandemic. She decorates the building for every holiday and often gathers the tenants (aged forty and up) to stand outside and sing "O Canada" on a Sunday morning. It's hard to say no to a cute little old lady in a Blue Jays jersey. (A few months ago she finally stopped the weekly stand-at-attention as she wryly stated, "I think they were placating me, Jacqueline.")

Her life hasn't been easy. She moved out of Toronto to live in cottage country for a while as a child and attended a one-room schoolhouse to avoid polio raging through the city. A tiny wooden cottage with no running water, no electricity or heating other than a small wood stove was home for a year. She lived through the Great Depression and lost her beloved brother Frankie, the closest sibling in age and personality, to the Second World War. She has long outlived all six of her other siblings, nursed her first young husband (while working full-time as a bank teller) through fourteen years of multiple myeloma before he died in his late fifties, and has buried her second husband, cousins, nieces, nephews, and her friends. Barring her progeny, everyone she loved and cared about throughout her life is long gone.

While a complicated woman in many respects with her own crosses to bear, Nanny is the epitome of a survivor.

For years I have read books on "The Blue Zones," following with fascination the areas of the world and means by which people lived much longer than the average lifespan. Okinawa, Sardinia, Icaria, Nicoya, Loma Linda … but I didn't have to look any farther than my own family. My grandmother has been asked time and again the secret to her long and healthy lifestyle. She doesn't drink alcohol, lives for Red Rose tea, eschews anything remotely fast food, hates medication and fruit equally, devours vegetables, and always, unfailingly, has three meals a day at a table fully set with real china. No standing at a counter scarfing down cold pizza for this lady. For as long as I can remember, she has walked, socialized, swum, cooked, baked, hosted card games with midnight feasts, gone to church, cheered on her favourite sports teams, read voraciously, and celebrated every holiday with verve. She stays remarkably social, physically active, and has a deep religious faith.

Blue Zone Nanny.

The woman doesn't stop. Her philosophy is "if you don't use it, you lose it." When she broke her pelvic bone five years ago, she was zipping up and down the hospital hallways on a walker every chance she had to get back into fighting shape—at which point the walker went out the window. She recently complained to me that she knocked something off the top of her refrigerator while cleaning it, while standing atop a ladder. The fact that it took me a second to wonder, "Wait a minute, Good God, why was she still climbing ladders?" – goes to show you how youthful she still seems.

Three years ago Sally and I were visiting Nanny and we decided to go for a walk downtown. Two hours of browsing later, we were ready for the fifteen-minute, uphill walk back. Halfway up the hill, it dawned on me that quite possibly my ninety-five-year-old grandmother might be tired (because, hey, I was), so I took her arm and started going more slowly. After a few minutes of this, she stopped, shook off my arm, stared me down, and asked, "Jacqueline, *why in the hell* are we going so slowly?"

Whatever was I thinking?

My grandfather died when I was in grade ten. My sister and I had gone to live with him and Nanny for a few months when our school had gone on strike and, during that time, I had gotten much closer to him. Standing by his hospital bed, overcome with emotion, I slipped out of the room and was staring out a window at the end of the hallway when Nanny joined me. She put her arm around me and uttered two words: "Chin up."

Chin up indeed.

It's not a bad philosophy, in the end.

✳ ✳ ✳

I don't ride horses. I mean—I have. Once in Cyprus, I even rode a racehorse. (Did they have no mild-mannered, pliant, plodding mares available?) "Get back on the horse" reverberated through my brain while riding. The statement presupposes that you are unceremoniously bucked off the horse, which didn't instill confidence. But it is a handy saying, reminding everyone to keep trying, face your fear, et cetera, et cetera.

I signed up to a course called "Outdoor

Education" when I was in grade eleven. Why, you might ask? My friends were taking it? My sister had taken it? My dad was a gym teacher? No good reason, really. Being a complete camping/outdoor novice, I was eager to test my mettle. The course culminated in a week-long sojourn on the Spanish River in northern Ontario, which has many canoeing routes for intermediate paddlers. We had had opportunities in advance to learn and practice different paddling techniques, how to portage, and lots of hiking time before we set out. I was paired with one of the two teachers. (This may speak to my extreme arm strength at the time.)

This was back in 1983, long before cell phones. It was only a day into the trip when we discovered a flood warning was in effect. Waters were high and the currents dangerous. We spent the rest of the week trying to get off of the river. Hours of portaging around unsafe waters were grueling; we paddled where we could and hiked the rest of the way. In the end, we made it a mere fifteen out of seventy kilometers that week.

We were a few days in when things got terrifying. Coming around a bend in the fast-flowing river, we saw a logjam up ahead with enormous logs everywhere. Voices imbued with urgency, the teachers yelled out instructions to have us draw and then paddle the canoes as fast as we could over to the bank. Most of us managed it. Two canoes tipped and boats, supplies, and students went hurtling down the water towards the mass of submerged logs and branches. One girl was trapped beneath a canoe until our teachers were able to grab her. Somehow all four students made it out. As a teacher now I can't imagine the sense of terror our leaders must have experienced, helplessly watching students in their charge racing towards danger.

Missing two tents, sleeping bags, dry clothes, food, paddles, and two canoes, we made camp. One of the teachers had hurt his ankle badly trying to pull a student out of the water, and one of the girls couldn't stop shaking. Within hours, hypothermia had set in; she couldn't tell us her name, and any talk was nonsensical. Even stripped down and warmed by body heat and fire, she didn't improve.

The teachers had a map depicting an old fishing camp many hiking hours away. Somehow the decision was made to send a male student (a cross-country runner) to take the map and run for help. He must have been terrified—sixteen years old, running through dense forest alone overnight with only a map and a flashlight, knowing how much was dependent upon him. I don't know why he went alone. Maybe no one else could keep up with him.

He ran ten kilometres through the night on a

wooded path to reach the camp. It had a big banner etched in wood at the entrance saying, "You've Made It." Our runner later recounted that he fell to his knees under the sign when he got there. He was truly heroic that night and rallied the cavalry to rescue us.

A helicopter evacuated the girl with hypothermia and the rest of us hiked to the camp behind a Cat that towed our canoes. Heading home the next day on the bus, we had seven hours with one cassette to listen to, so every word of Meatloaf's *Bat Out of Hell* was etched in our brains forever by the time we rolled into town backwards. It's amazing that the opening strains alone of "Paradise by the Dashboard Light" don't cause us all to experience PTSD.

As we prepared to exit the bus outside the school, one of the teachers asked us not to embellish the story because, honestly, no embellishment was needed.

The course was cancelled shortly thereafter and wasn't reinstated until many years later. As an adult sharing drinks and reminiscing with several of the people who had been on the trip, I realized just how terrified everyone had been. Only a couple of people had ever wanted to venture out in a canoe again, and most admitted that they were so traumatized by the experience they were happy to never paddle again.

As I was closing in on thirty, my boyfriend convinced me to give it another go, so, after another year spent living in a hot desert, I cautiously stepped foot into a canoe for the first time in thirteen years. We ventured out onto a lake (no rapids), and as we paddled along, I spotted a large group of canoeists heading towards us. I kid you not; it was one of my Outdoor Ed teachers, leading a new group of students. The course had just been reinstated.

You can't make this stuff up.

I enjoyed canoeing on my second go-around, although I never did come around to fast-moving water. Portaging is painful, frankly, and I can live out the remainder of my life quite happily without ever sleeping on another Thermarest. Now I have my trusty kayak, in which I paddle peacefully along the shores of Lake Huron, enjoying my solitude and gorgeous sunsets.

I may not have gotten back up on the racing horse, but I definitely mounted a pony. And it was worth it.

* * *

No Ewing Christmas is complete without the obligatory viewing of *Home Alone*. That Kevin was a wily one all right. He may have hidden under the blankets briefly but soon after hit full hard-ass mode; Marv and Harry didn't stand a chance. I have had several experiences with interlopers over the years but haven't handled them with the aplomb that Kevin did.

In my second year of university, I lived in the basement of a dilapidated house. Oh, the glory days of student housing. I had to walk on a board over an ever-present six-inch puddle of water to get to my room. It was lovely. Two roommates were housed on the main level and three more on the top floor. One night I ventured up from my hovel at around eleven-thirty after getting off the phone (back then, you had to wait until after eleven for cheap phone time) to see what everyone was up to. The kitchen and living room were dim, and I could see a male figure sitting on our couch. My roommate Liz's new boyfriend was coming to visit that weekend, but I hadn't met him yet. I walked over to the couch, perched on the arm, and, being the friendly sort, leaned my elbow on the back of the couch and said, "Hey, you must be Mark. Nice to meet you!"

The male grunted in response.

Well, I thought indignantly to myself, *Mark isn't super friendly.*

Upon closer inspection, I realized that Mark was quite a bit older—years and years older, actually—

and rather scruffy and unkempt. He leaned over the coffee table and picked up a bill that was sitting there. "Jacqueline Ewing," he read aloud in a slow, halting voice, followed by our address.

Mark was flat-out strange.

Aim higher, Liz, aim higher!

I cautiously extricated myself from my too-cozy perch and went upstairs to find Sandra and my other good friend, Nancy. I plopped down on Nancy's bed.

"Liz's boyfriend seems kind of weird," I said. "Where is she, anyways?"

Nancy looked at me like I was crazy and replied that they had both left over an hour ago to head out to a bar. Nancy, Sandra, and I stared at each other. Silence.

"So," I said carefully, "then who's the old guy on the couch …?"

We crept down the stairs to peek, Nancy first. She turned on the light, let out a blood-curdling scream, tossed Sandra and me aside, and leapt upstairs, two steps at a time to Sandra's closet. We raced after her, slammed the bedroom door behind us, and tried in vain to block it. We picked up the phone to call 911 and our roommate Karen was on the line wanting to know what in the bloody hell was going on. Her bedroom was directly off the living room. She decided that since he hadn't murdered her or any of us yet, she would go talk to Not-Mark. As much as the rest of us wanted to hide in the closet, we decided that valour was the better part of discretion and joined her for backup. It turned out that Not-Mark was just a drunk/strung-out-creepy guy who had wandered into our unlocked house. After a few minutes of a politely veneered, "Get your ass out of here" conversation, he left. He'd been enjoying some KFC and had kindly left a bucket behind in the kitchen for us to enjoy.

Actual Mark was a great guy. He and Liz are still happily together and have a beautiful family to boot.

They never eat chicken.

Years later, I encountered another interloper while residing in Kuwait. Living on the fifth floor of an apartment building, I revelled in having my own space. What made it even better was the fact that the rest of the building was filled with fellow teachers from the school. Close my door = privacy. Open my door = socialize.

That day I had just walked into my apartment with a load of groceries. The kitchen was in a straight line from the door, through the living room and down the hall, at the back of the apartment. I hadn't locked the door behind me as my arms were full, but I had closed it. As I was setting the groceries down on the counter, I heard a bang on my door. Assuming it was Tessa (who lived next door), I called out "Come on in," as I walked towards the entrance.

The door swung open and ... I knew. A strange man was standing there and just from the way that he looked at me, I knew.

I tried to slam the door shut but he stuck his foot in the doorway and pushed his way in. I remember desperately thinking, don't run, you'll just get deeper into the apartment and farther from the hallway. He reached out and grabbed me.

You know those nightmares that you sometimes have where you freeze and can't even scream? Well, that didn't happen to me. I screamed bloody murder, spitting and hitting as he was gripping me. Thankfully Tessa and her husband Drew were home and heard the noise. They were chatting in their kitchen when they heard yelling and quickly realized it was in English and coming from next door. I have no memory of words coming out of my mouth, but evidently, I swear like a sailor when push comes to shove. Drew, although small in stature, was mighty in spirit. He threw open his door and bellowed. Scary Man let go of me, spun around and out the door and ran down the stairs with Drew in hot pursuit. He got away in the end, never to be seen again.

I don't think I slept a wink that night. Word spread, and the next day I had several fellow teachers randomly decide to "pop in," ostensibly to visit my grade one class. They just happened to have a storybook in hand or a class activity planned that they were itching to try out. At one point my principal came in and found me sound asleep in my rocking chair while a buddy was leading the class in song. My yearly teacher assessment had been successfully completed and filed earlier in the year so, drool aside, all was well.

Tessa and I had had another encounter a couple of years earlier, during our first year in Kuwait. At the time, the city was slowly coming back to life but had a long way to go. The Hungry Bunny was the only restaurant open the first month. Taxis were in short supply. We had taken to getting around by flagging down Wanettes, basically independent taxis in the form of pickup trucks that charged 1KD (Kuwaiti dinar) for a drive. One night Tessa and I flagged down a white pickup truck and hopped in. We explained where we were going but very soon realized that we were not, in fact, headed in the right direction. We were headed outside of town (and into the desert).

The driver, being ahem, "handily" able to multitask, was pulling up his dishdasha around his waist and grabbing the Kleenex box closer to him. All preparations in place, he reached back and started grabbing Tessa, trying to pull her closer. I was yanking her other arm and much screaming and yelling ensued.

Alas, there was to be no "happy ending" for Taxi Guy. At the next red light Tessa was able to shake free. We jumped out of the truck and ran like our lives depended upon it.

Sharing an apartment in Mexico my first year with a lovely girl also included her two cats. We lived on the third floor and had a balcony overlooking a little courtyard. One afternoon I was alone and taking a nap when I awoke to the sounds of the felines howling. I got up to explore, following the sounds which led me to the balcony. I stepped out and froze face-to-face with a man who had one leg over the edge of the balcony. The walls were interlocking brick with tiny spaces in between and he had literally scaled the wall like Peter Parker.

Silence. It was a (ha) Mexican standoff.

A lone leaf fluttered to the ground.

All I could think of in the moment was how to ask him in Spanish what he was doing. My frozen brain was not cooperating. Instead of running back inside and locking the door like any sane person, I put my hand on my hip and snarled (probably quivered, but it's my story, so I'm sticking with snarled), "Qu'est-ce que tu fais?"

I always knew that my high school years of French would not go amiss.

Climbing Man stared me down but, perhaps not being a Francophone, didn't answer. He simply pulled his leg back over the ledge and slowly and carefully proceeded to make his way to the ground.

I went in, locked the door, and resumed my nap.

Au revoir, Spanish Spidey.

After my first incident with Chicken Man (aka Not-Mark), I struggled to move past the fear. Even though he turned out to be a harmless drunk in the end, the fact that he had been inside our home stuck with me. I felt vulnerable and violated.

That summer, I was working behind a small bar at a pizza place in our neighbouring town. A young Polish boy was the dishwasher there and was a quiet but hardworking employee who always had a shy smile to share. His father would walk down to meet him at the end of each shift. He would sit quietly at the bar, nursing his beer, waiting for his son before their evening stroll home. The connection between the two was strong, and it was a pleasure to be in their company. He seemed like a bit of a wise soul and emanated compassion. He spoke little, but when he did, his words carried weight.

One night it was just the two of us, and somehow, I ended up telling him about our experience, how it had left me more shaken than I had expected, and that I was struggling to move past it. He looked at me quietly and then, in his thick accent, told me that he was very sorry I had gone through this. He expressed that fear should not win, that I should lay my fear down and walk away, otherwise, I would always be carrying it. *Sometimes*, he said, *bad things in life happen for no good reason, and we have to set them down on the side of the road to move forwards.*

The right words at the right time said in the right way by the right person.

Kevin had a battle plan. Kevin had props. Kevin had weapons. Kevin even had a zip line. But me? I had a gentle Polish sage at a bar.

✳ ✳ ✳

As a small-town high school teacher, Dad became close friends with many of his peers. So, when one of his fellow teachers was celebrating a birthday, Dad was in. Heading over to a bar a few miles away, the men celebrated with drinks and ... cough ... entertainment. An older woman was "performing" at good ole bar in a neighbouring town, and the men got to chatting her up. She confessed that she had secretly always wanted to be a teacher but didn't know how to start the process. She wondered if it was too late. The men vociferously voiced the opinion that the ship hadn't sailed, and that there was lots of help and information out there. "In fact," offered the birthday boy, "why don't you pop by the school and I will personally give you a tour and some pointers?"

Monday rolled around. The men were relaxing in the staff room, Dad with his eyes closed briefly in the corner, when the secretary walked in. With a thinly veiled look of scorn on her face, she glanced down at Birthday Boy with a sniff and told him that he had a visitor. She then escorted their dancing friend into the room.

According to the men, who shared this story with me after Dad passed away, all of them turned puce, mumbled excuses, and, tails between their legs, escaped as quickly as possible. This left the poor woman standing alone, embarrassed, and the receiver of several blistering glances from other staff members.

One lone reveller stayed. Dad gave the lady the promised tour of the school and then handed her over politely to the school counsellor who would advise her on next steps.

The men told me that Dad hadn't wanted them to chat her up at the bar that night and had actively tried to dissuade them from inviting her to the school. All of which had fallen on deaf/drunk ears. And yet ... he was the only one who, perhaps to his detriment, faced the fire and stepped up when she took them up on their invitation.

Curtis Owen Ewing, 1940-2005.

It seems like a common practice to bestow sainthood upon everyone once they pass away. Dad wasn't a saint, but he was a genuinely good, kind man, and you would be hard-pressed to find anyone who disagreed with that assessment. He hailed from a long line of the Ewing/Locke Clan without a mean or judgmental bone in their bodies, so he came by it honestly.

Along with being my father, Dad was also a kindred spirit.

I had the house to myself one wintry weekend afternoon. Dad was outside clearing snow off the roof. Well, roofs really—three of them at ascending levels on our red-brick abode. Curled up on the couch in the family room reading a book (as was my norm), I suddenly heard a crash and strangled cry. Rushing outside, I discovered my dad lying with the ladder on top of him. It had slipped off of the third story, sending him hurtling to the ground. With the help of a little snow carpeting the concrete driveway, Dad had escaped with merely a broken finger.

Entering my physics class a few days later, I readied myself for a test. Papers were handed out as I was up sharpening my pencil near the front of the room. Chortles emerged from my fellow students behind me. Curiosity aroused, I headed back to my seat and picked up the test. The first question read, "If Curtis Ewing fell from the third roof at a velocity of _m per second squared, hit the second roof at an angle of _ and bounced at a velocity of _m per second , at what…"

Did I mention that we live in a small town?

I suspect that, had this happened in the present day, Dad's epic fall would have become a meme on social media.

Apple/Tree.

Die-hard Leaf fan, skipper of two grades in elementary school, executor of the smooth but deadly tennis forehand, lifelong runner, passer down of the long, skinny-legged gene, jive-dancing maestro, crossword puzzle aficionado, lover of long walks and bike rides, keen sports-card collector, champion napper, adroit stove-top popcorn maker, painstakingly slow but avid reader, connoisseur of the ice cream/butterscotch syrup/peanut concoction, preserver of photographic family memories, ping-pong virtuoso, creator of the "climb up and dive through the tiny family room window when locked out" maneuver, neighbourhood bar-setter for last to take down outside Christmas lights, steady-handed batter-pourer of letter-shaped pancakes (L,J,D,D), master air-conditioner-drop-per-out-of-second-story-window, gourmet Hamburger Soup chef extraordinaire, Bjorn Borg-esque catcher of attic bats, initiator of the "Family Fun" runs around the high school track, expert judge of the oatmeal cookie par excellence, but most of all, loving friend, son, brother, husband, father, and grandfather.

Dad retired at the age of fifty-five. He had what he considered the best five years of his life in retirement, happily partaking in his many hobbies and activities. At sixty he was diagnosed with multiple myeloma, the disease that my maternal grandfather had died of. He passed away a month before his sixty-fifth birthday.

When my father was five, he had his tonsils removed on the kitchen table of his home. My uncle remembers sitting out on the front steps, gagging from waves of ether that permeated the air. Dad had tetanus a few years later and almost died, and then, as a teenager, was diagnosed with narcolepsy, which would plague him for the remainder of his life. He chose gym teacher as a career path over his first choice of accountant as he thought that the movement would be a better fit. He always said that he didn't expect to live a long life, and sadly his words were prophetic.

Dad had gone downhill by Christmas of 2004. We knew that all treatments had stopped, and it was palliative care at that point. He didn't like to talk about it, in true Curt-like fashion, because he didn't want to make anyone else feel bad. He was using a walker, depressed, a little angry, not getting out of bed or his armchair much, and rarely wanted to engage.

I came back to visit in mid-March; being off on maternity leave with Finn I had a bit of freedom. I had brought some funny movies along with me in hopes of cheering Dad up a bit, at least for a couple of hours.

But when I opened the front door, I had the surprise of my life. Dad was there. No walker. Not hunched over. Downright sprightly. A huge smile (and when Dad smiled at you, you felt like you were the only person in the room), a giant hug, and "Jac!" That night we all sat down at the kitchen table, had a meal just like old times with lots of laughing and chatting, and then Mom, Dad, and I sat up in the living room for several hours after dinner talking about everything and nothing. Dad had always dreamed about travelling to Vancouver Island so he brought out his maps and talked animatedly about a trip. We looked at old photos too, but mostly, we just had a night that was ... normal.

I had my dad back that evening.

The next morning Dad was rushed to the hospital. He wasn't a complainer, so when he couldn't bear it, we knew he was truly hurting. He died later that night. He was terrified of lingering in the hospital for months in chronic pain, so in the end, I'm glad that he didn't have to endure that. The last words he said were a slightly bewildered, "I'm surrounded," to the empty room around him. He lost the ability to speak after a few hours but still seemed able to hear. We all had the opportunity to tell him what an exceptional father/husband he had been to us and how loved he was. Mom told him it was okay to go, that we would be all right and ... he did.

Going home and seeing the maps that we'd been looking at on the coffee table, the bowl of nuts he was eating, and the glass sitting by his recliner was surreal. The TV shows continued to play with their canned laughter. Joggers chatted between huffs and puffs on their daily run down the street. The garbage truck still stopped out front for its weekly pickup. The world marched onward.

Life. Death.

I struggled with this for quite a while afterwards. I remember driving in downtown Toronto shortly after Dad's death and passing people swarming by on the streets with their briefcases and suits and wanting to scream at them that life was short, too short to waste it by working nonstop. I might have been arrested for harassment, though, so I'm glad that my baser nature didn't take over. Orange clashes with my hair.

Grieving is hard. It's not something that happens overnight. Grief catches you unaware sometimes, just when you think you have it licked. The good thing about grief though, is that it abates over time. Memories become less raw eventually and can even bring you joy.

Dad shared that the worst thing about dying was thinking about the family gatherings he was going to miss. I like to think that he gets to see some of them and is happy with how we're all doing. He's never far from our thoughts. He left a huge hole in our lives when he passed, which is a testament to his character. My mom ended up getting married again years after his death, to one of Dad's old friends and colleagues, Ken. We love Ken dearly and know that Dad would approve.

My siblings and I raise a glass and eat an oatmeal cookie annually on Dad's birthday. He would like that.

Our Christmas lights stay up year-round.

✳ ✳ ✳

The show *Lassie* aired for many a year, but I only watched it for the last two or so years. Timmy was always safe with good ole Lassie on the lookout. She was unfailing in her ability to locate lost children or adults alike and always ensured they returned to safety.

One March Break, Mike and I had taken Molly and Finn (then aged six and three respectively) on a day trip to a butterfly conservatory. The roads were mostly devoid of snow on the return trip—much better than on the ride down—but were still covered in patches. We were all happy and a little tired after a lovely day away. Finn was sound asleep in his car seat, and Molly was quietly looking at the scenery. Coming over a hill, about an hour and a quarter from home, nodding my head in time to the song on the radio, peacefully gazing out the window, we unexpectedly hit a large patch of built-up snow and lost control of the car, fishtailing all over the highway. In a blink of an eye, we flew off the road, flipped and landed upside-down in a field, dangling by our seatbelts.

Stunned, we were silent for a few seconds with just the sound of the engine running and the same song quietly playing. My first coherent thought was the kids aren't crying. Why aren't the kids crying? Seconds felt like hours until they both answered our frantic call. Just then we heard a knock on the car window. In our dazed state we saw a man wearing a shirt with a Search and Rescue logo on it leaning down. All I could think was, "My goodness –

they're so fast." It turns out that Rescue Fellow was driving behind us and had seen us go off the road.

Although the car was totaled, we all escaped unscathed. Had a car been coming the other way as we slid across the yellow line, or had we hit a tree/hydro pole as we flipped across the field, it would have been a different story.

We were exceptionally lucky that afternoon in March. Our Search and Rescue version of Lassie was a kindly man who helped us out, contacted the police, and made sure we were okay. My friend Paul was Lassie 2.0 as he hopped in his car and drove without hesitation to pick us up and take us home.

We weren't lost in a well but we needed saving that day. Everybody needs saving once in a while. Lassies come in all shapes and sizes, thankfully, because when the ground beneath us gives way, they're all we've got.

If you haven't got one, get a Lassie. Or two.

Even better, be one.

✳ ✳ ✳

I'm quite fond of my breasts. They're rather perky for a woman of my advanced years. I'm currently reading the book *The Subtle Art of Not Giving a F*ck*, and I realize that this is probably not something to which I should allocate any time or pride, and yet, there it is.

Perky though they may be, my breasts are not terribly bright. They are, in fact, incredibly dense. Many a mammogram has resulted in an ultrasound followed by a biopsy to rule out anything serious, and after a while, I didn't even blink at the process.

One particular biopsy was tricky. I was poked and prodded so much I looked like a piece of cheesecloth and couldn't stop bleeding. The upside was that the doctor who did it was a mighty handsome one and charismatic to boot, so I easily agreed to more pokes. The man could have asked if he could put the needle in my eye instead, and I would have asked demurely, "Would you prefer the left or the right?" as I twirled a hair strand nonchalantly with my finger. I was also frantically trying to recall how many days it had been since I last shaved my underarms, so, between the distractions, I wasn't even remotely worried.

The next day was a delight. Picture teaching in front of a grade six class, writing on the board when you hear a whisper from the students that stops your heart. Looking down I discovered that blood was seeping through my bandages and my pastel shirt on full display.

Ms. Ewing will be right back. Read quietly.

Getting the call that my results were indicative

of cancer and a lumpectomy was scheduled was a bit of a shock. The surgery went smoothly, and I was released the same day. My mom had taken me there, waited all day, and driven me home. Now, my mom doesn't use public bathrooms. This is not an exaggeration. The woman has been on eight-hour flights and still won't use them.

She's a veritable camel in the bladder department. To help her avoid public washroom activity, she refuses to eat or drink, so by the time I was ready to go home, Mom hadn't had so much as a sip of water. It was dark out, and Mom isn't the best driver under the best of circumstances. She finally passed her test the third time when she promised the instructor she would only drive in our small town. She did break this vow periodically and, witnessing her backing down Toronto's Gardiner Expressway on-ramp, waving blithely to the other drivers, is an experience I would like to erase from my memory. So even in my drug-induced state after my surgery, I was nervous. It was a long forty-five minutes home. At one point, Mom, thinking it was still a four-lane highway, was driving on the wrong side of the road. I convinced her to stop and buy herself a snack and, while she was inside, called my sister. I remember sleepily saying that I had survived the surgery but wasn't sure I'd make the drive home.

Sitting in the hospital room waiting to hear my results a week or so later, the doctor didn't keep me in suspense. Within seconds of walking into the room, he told me that my tumour had been benign. He continued to say that he had just left another room with another patient, a woman the same age, who had been told the opposite news and that I was the lucky one.

A roll of the dice? Why her and not me? Who knows, but it did make me pause and take stock. The words "Life is short. Be happy" reverberated in my brain in giant flashing neon letters.

Time has passed, and my perky girls are decidedly less so, but I'm still here and that—well, *that* I give a f*ck about.

✶ ✶ ✶

Gwyneth and Chris consciously uncoupled. They set the bar high for divorced parents everywhere—damn them and their perfect Hollywood lives. Divorce sucks, especially when there are young hearts involved. Nobody gets married thinking that it won't last, so it's the end of a dream for two people, and a seismic change for children.

I can't say that I wasn't warned.

Mike's mom, Edna, suffered from dementia later in life, as can unfortunately happen to the best of us, and was living in a nursing home. I would stop by to visit sometimes while walking home from the school I was working at. She had had a brother named Hector, long gone by then, who had been married to Jeanine. In Edna's mind, I was often Jeanine. There was no rhyme or reason to it, so I just went with the flow. Jeanine had been a hair-dresser, and the odd "wash and cut" was requested, so I had to explain that I had forgotten my shears. (Considering my self-trimmed, crooked bangs over the years, it was really the kindest thing I could do.)

One afternoon I was chatting with Edna when she started talking to "Jeanine" about her children. After a few minutes of me casually nodding to off-hand comments about a couple of her grown chil-dren, she turned, shook her head, and said wryly, "Now, that Jackie and Mike, *they're* never going to make it."

Prescient Edna.

Learning to live in a house on my own was an adjustment. I discovered that, although a rock star at hanging with the kids, reading my book, and keeping the interior of the place looking good, I failed miserably at outdoor maintenance. My neighbours were thankfully forgiving of my ever-increasing love of dandelions and three-foot weeds, but driving through a foot of snow on my regularly unplowed driveway made parking a constant adventure.

I soon learned that there were other roles that Mike had taken on that were rather foreign to me.

One weekend I spontaneously decided to take the kids to a nearby mountain village resort. Zip-lining, rock climbing, bopping to a surprise performance by David Wilcox (at least I bopped; "Riverboat Fantasy" and I are more than casual friends), and beaver tail sampling kept us busy. We rounded off the day by browsing through a toy shop. A plastic pair of handcuffs were chosen, paid for, and bagged and we were ready to head home. Molly, being old and tall enough, sat beside me in the front seat and Finn was in the back. They decided to test out the cuffs and their hands were suspended in the air between the rows as we sat at a red light.

Seconds later flashing lights appeared behind me and before I knew what was happening, found myself being pulled over by a man in blue. Steely-eyed and immune to a feeble attempt at flirting, he demanded to know why there were children hand-cuffed in my vehicle. He was ready to haul me out of the car and cuff me too, until he realized that the shackles were plastic and the kids were giggling. My toy store receipt sealed the deal.

Crisis averted, I let out a sigh of relief. Just as I was about to pull out on the road again, my officer of the law was back. It appeared that my license plate sticker was out of date. My valiant attempts to explain that I was newly separated and that my ex had always taken care of said stickers fell on deaf ears (as, truly, they should have).

Those bloody handcuffs ended up costing me a hundred and thirty dollars. They broke in two days, never to be used again.

I learned to renew my sticker. I hired a neighbourhood teen to mow and shovel. The many other roles that Mike had undertaken slowly made their way into my repertoire, although I continued to subscribe to the "open tool box and take out cheque book instead of tools" philosophy of home maintenance. I learned to navigate my life as a single woman once again, albeit this time with two young children. The first Christmas that the three of us picked out, brought home, lugged in, and set up a real tree, I felt invincible.

Mike and I got together quickly when we first met. Instead of "*He had me at hello,*" he had me when he ate my novice attempt at chocolate pie without a single grimace (so tricky to tell the salt from the sugar when baking).

We had a lot of happy times over our years together. Mike helped me to conquer some fears, opened my life up to new experiences and alternate ways of viewing things, and very often made me laugh. Highly intelligent, driven, musical, and out-doorsy, he passed a lot of traits and talents along to his kids. Our marriage brought those two beautiful children into the world and our lives, and for that, we're both eternally thankful.

This doesn't mean that a lot of pain and stress didn't join us along the way. We didn't manage our uncoupling nearly as well as the Paltrow/Martin model, but ... we did the best we could. Time has passed, and we're both happy with our lives and in great relationships. The kids are good; life is good.

Viva la Vida.

✹ ✹ ✹

"Here's a story."

Brady Bunch, my ass. Carol and Mike might have made it all look as easy as pie but I'd like to have seen them blend their family without the help of the unflappable, neutral, take-care-of-the-grunt-work Alice.

I read. I read everything. When I'm trying to figure something out, I research the crap out of it. Once Dave and I decided to take the plunge and move in together, I dove into the printed word on "blending" with every fibre of my controlling being. Pitfalls, you ask? Where should I start?

False expectations? I could recite them to the

letter. Statistics rolled off my tongue. Suggestions to make the venture easier on the kids? Let me count the ways.

Oh, I was prepared and passed along my new-found knowledge verbatim to Dave, a lot of which came in handy when specific situations arose. I was open-eyed and unfazed by the seventy percent divorce rate of second families. I serenely accepted the average four-to-seven-year period for family blending. Not even the fact that we would have four kids between the grey-hair-inducing ages of eleven and fifteen caused me to falter. Knowing that we had each been divorced many years before meeting was in our favour, at least. Dating for two years before moving in together was, too. Living together for a year before marrying also helped. And giving the kids a whole lot of bio-family time, especially in the first couple of years, definitely made a difference. Dave, well Dave calmly took in all aforementioned information and, in true Dave-like manner, proceeded to be his unflappable self, steering our boat safely through the waters, however choppy they might become.

One night, before we moved into our new house together, we were all in Dave's backyard. Dave and I were sitting on a loveseat talking about the impending move while the kids were on the trampoline. One of the pitfalls mentioned in my research was the concern of romantic relationships developing between the children. We considered the issue briefly, and then both agreed, "Nah, that's not something we have to worry about." There had been no sign of this in the two years we had been dating. And at that *exact moment,* we heard Braeden call out, "Molly, Molly! Get on your hands and knees!"

I do not recall Greg saying this to Marcia.

Moving into a "new to us" five-bedroom home within the same neighbourhood that we'd all lived in previously helped to start our family off on a clean, yet familiar slate. A giant finished basement with a pool table, ping-pong table, foosball, TV, and even (for later years) a bar, helped. Putting up a basketball net and enough of a court to throw a three-pointer for our basketball-obsessed boys didn't hurt.

Being a teacher in a small town, I had taught many of the kids' friends. This was a good thing in lots of ways as I knew them all and was comfortable having them around. It also had its drawbacks.

Dave's dog Murphy has a tendency to chew underwear—specifically mine. (We're very close.)

One afternoon Braeden had a few of his buddies over in the backyard and I heard him call out, "Jackie, Murphy's got your underwear again."

I regally walked through the boys, casually

nodding to my former students as I stooped to wrestle the underwear out of Doggo's mouth. Any lingering pride I had went out the window as I saw that he had grabbed my granny period underwear out of the dirty clothes basket. It's hard to look cool when you're wrangling blood-stained giant cotton panties out from a romping fifty-pound dog in front of grade nine boys.

The kids adjusted to the move quite well overall and a year later Dave and I were married. They all willingly participated in a choreographed dance to "We Are Family" at the tiny reception, complete with giant pictures of Dave's dog and my cat.

Ah ... the dog and the cat. Let me just say that they did not blend easily nor swiftly. Dog wanted to eat Cat. Cat had to live in the basement for a year and a half. Daughter staged a revolt. Dog got a shock collar. Dog believes Cat has superpowers. Cat now reigns supreme.

The four-to-seven-year blending timeline seems accurate. We've lived together six years so far, and time has certainly helped. A reserved politeness has long since passed, and the kids are natural with each other and with Dave and me. We have staged (especially during Covid lockdown) photo scavenger hunts, Saturday night cook-offs, "How Well Do You Know Your Steps" Jeopardy games, family game nights, backyard movies, and gone on some great family trips over the years. We've even been known to car dance once or twice. What makes me the happiest, though, is knowing that the kids often text/Facetime each other when they're apart. When they choose to hang out together on their own, I realize just how far we've all come.

It hasn't always been easy. Children want their parents together. No one really wants to move in with another brood, and there have been bumps and tears along the way. Blending a family is not for the faint of heart. You are naturally going to feel compelled to take sides with your bio family, and at times, Dave and I have felt utterly torn and on the defence. Dave is the most easygoing of men, however, and all four kids are, without a doubt, great people. Each of them is kindhearted, intelligent, fun, and open, and that has made all the difference. The fact that we didn't get a single "You're not my mom/dad!" or "I hate you!" screamed at either of us is a miracle and speaks volumes about their natures. I wouldn't have wanted to go through this with any other group. I feel confident that, despite some ups and downs, all four children are coming out of this experience with more people to love them in the world, and that can't be a bad thing.

As tricky as it's been at times, most of the experience has been genuinely wonderful.

I'm so glad that I got back up and on the marital horse again.

Dave and I knew and it was much more than a hunch.

Step aside, Carol and Mike.

LIFE LESSON #8

JUST KEEP
GETTING BACK UP.

The Dead Sea is a handy place to fall into (as long as you keep your eyes and mouth closed). You really do pop right back up to the surface. Can't keep a good man/woman down. If only life were like that.

Some people are born with resiliency and manage to survive, rise above their life circumstances, and change their path, while others increase it gradually. The School of Hard Knocks certainly helps you to build it bit by bit. Tough times are going to happen; there's no avoiding pain or struggle. You're going to need that "get back up again" skill a lot if you're lucky enough to live a decently long life.

I deal with my crap by venting to my friends and family. I vent a lot. They're cheap counsellors. I have also gone to actual counsellors, and they've helped too. I jump on my mini-trampoline (don't judge until you've tried it – thirty minutes on that sucker helps get rid of stress) and sit in my sauna. I walk. I ensconce myself in one of my sister's beautiful beach chairs, listening to the waves and, when the spirit moves me, meander along the shore in my kayak. I curl up on my covered deck, listening to the rain while I read my book. I dance. I instantly feel lighter just remembering dancing upon the shores of Lake Huron at two in the morning with friends to "Two Princes" after a night of revelry at our favourite watering hole. I listen to music; the right song can change my mood more adeptly than anything else.

Sometimes I try to help someone. Often, I just need to spend time with people or watch shows that make me laugh. I try to control (shocker) what I can by making plans. I've been known to dull the pain with a barrel full of chips and dip. Sometimes I need to forgive others or forgive myself to move forwards. I let myself have days when I'm not Pollyanna and everything seems difficult. I try to remember to be grateful—and I have much to be grateful for. Eventually, I remind myself what I've gone through and get back up.

I may not be June in Gilead, but I'm stronger than I look.

A pandemic that swept across the globe changed the way we all live, from the youngest to the oldest in every nook and cranny in the world. It's brought monumental challenges and suffering. It's overwhelming realizing that those daily death statistics represent actual people. For the most part, I stay hopeful and try to remember that change, whether good or bad, is a part of life, and the only way past it is to move through it. This, too, shall pass.

Time really does, if not heal, temper the pain.

The world can be a challenging place to navigate. But, navigate it we must; there really isn't any other choice after all.

So, figure out what works for you when the sh*t hits the fan (because it will).

And ... chin up.

CHAPTER NINE

"NOLITE TE BASTARDES CARBORUNDORUM"

I should have been called Grey. I mean, why not? Apple is a name. So is Bear. And Gravity. And even (God help the poor child) X Æ A-12. Grey seems reasonable to me. It's not that I feel colourless—I'm a multicoloured special snowflake. It's more that I don't see things in black or white. Like, ever. I can always see two sides to an issue. This sounds great in theory but is kind of crappy in reality. It's hard to take a stand or voice your opinion when you're never one hundred percent sure what your opinion is. It's entirely possible that I just don't want to deal with defending my position so taking the middle road saves me from angst.

In short, I care too much about what other people think.

Now, Pink on the other hand—Pink is a fine name. It's one of the first colours to be picked from the crayon box. It's vibrant and stands out, just like the aptly named singer. Pink is a bad ass. She doesn't seem to give two hoots about other people's opinions and she definitely walks to the beat of her own drum. I admire that. The fact that she can also perform aerial acrobatics while singing shows that she flies in the face of naysayers everywhere. You don't like what she does or says? She shrugs.

One might even hear her say, "So What?"

✳ ✳ ✳

Many years ago I attended a session on integration at a teachers' conference while teaching in a private school in the city. I unwittingly committed a faux pas and went off script from the party line. I didn't even know there was a line so please, fellow educators, forgive me in advance.

We were all gathered in a small room, about twenty-five of us. The workshop was about tackling the issue of integrating students with intense behaviour needs into the classroom full time. We began the session by stating our thoughts on the matter on a piece of paper without writing our names on it. I pondered for a moment and then wrote something along the lines of, "While I agree that it may be in the best interest of the student to be integrated, I'm concerned that the learning and class environment of the other students would be negatively impacted, and feel that their needs should be taken into consideration also, which is why I support *partial* integration with support."

After we wrote our statements, we were told to crumple our papers and toss them around the room, snowball fight-style. I confidently crunched mine up and tossed it gamely. The leader then proceeded with her talk. Within minutes I was clear on the party line: *FULL* INTEGRATION FOR ALL NO MATTER THE COST.

As the facilitator's talk continued, I felt my spine slowly start to curve. I was full-on slouched in my chair by the end of her speech. I could confidently predict what was going to happen to the snowball by now. Could I zip out for a bathroom break? Feign illness? Swoon with light-headedness? While these thoughts were reverberating in my brain, we were asked to grab the paper ball nearest to us, open it up and read it aloud. The first twenty-two or so were remarkably similar and stated, with minuscule variations, an opinion validating the party line. Everyone would clap vigorously and nod in agreement. My head was bobbing up and down with enthusiasm, and no one put their hands together more loudly than Grey.

At long last, my paper was opened and read out to the group.

Silence.

In my head I heard, "Do not pass Go. Do not collect $200. Go directly to jail."

Horror-stricken faces turned to one another—mine being one of the first. "My God," my face read, "Can you believe this? What simpleton wrote that?" Eyes rolling, I'm sure that I muttered, "Wing-nut!" under my breath to the person beside me while using my finger to draw circles around the side of my tilted head.

The organizer said ... nothing. The participants said ... nothing. At least thirty seconds passed with complete silence. Finally, she took a deep breath and proceeded with her talk as if nothing had happened, ignoring the final few paper snowballs. There was no discussion of this alternative, ostensibly ludicrous opinion.

Beneath contempt.

I noticed the tightly permed lady beside me glance down with a sniff at my pen. My purple pen whose ink was now visible for all and sundry to see on the white sheet that had been held aloft in the air.

The offending pen was strategically and quickly hidden in my bag using the good ole yawn and stretch gambit. I then, as the dad in one of my favourite books, *The Glass Castle*, says, did The Great Skedaddle and motored on out of there the second the workshop ended.

I stand by my snowball statement—if only in my head. I also switched to unremarkable blue Bic pens for all future workshops.

✶ ✶ ✶

Job interviews are not my forte. I worry so much about how I will come across that I tend to freeze up. One afternoon I was being interviewed for a teaching job by a highly renowned principal and a vice principal. I wanted them to see just how talented, knowledgeable, and professional I was. In short, I wanted to impress them. I wanted them to think highly of me, even if I didn't end up getting the position. The interview was going along half-decently, then the principal asked me to describe my literacy program. Now, I am an English major whose passion is teaching literacy. I knew all the current buzzwords and had years of experience with which to support my answer.

Instead, I said, "We read. And we write."

Yes, teachers everywhere, I said, *We read, and we write.*

The admin team sat there blank-faced, waiting for me to expand upon my answer. And I said … nothing. I nodded a few times. I smiled. I admired the office plant. I brought up the weather.

I didn't get the position.

The interview that did grant me my first job within our board was the opposite experience. I was sick with a cold and lacking the energy to worry about my chances of getting the job, let alone be nervous. I politely refrained from shaking hands when I walked in, explaining that I didn't want to pass anything along. I was too exhausted to care much about what they thought of me and … I nailed it. I was just me, and that was enough.

Meryl Streep pronounced that, "The minute you start caring about what other people think, is the minute you stop being yourself."

Pro tip: Only interview for a new job when you're too tired to care.

✷ ✷ ✷

Luna from *Harry Potter* is my hero. She self-assuredly handles name-calling, having her things taken, and people avoiding her because she's different. Throughout it all, she remains irrevocably herself, neither bitter nor vengeful. She continues living her cheerful, dreamy, Luna-ish life, giving little weight to the opinions of others. I recognize that she is a fictional character but know that there are actual Luna-like peeps out there in real life. I applaud them.

It's a pubescent jungle out there, people; fore-warned is forearmed.

My teeth, coupled with my long, thin arms and legs, were the bane of my late elementary school existence. Grades six, seven, and eight were the worst years, and during that time my self-esteem took a nosedive. Bucky was my nickname, among other variations on the theme during those pre-braces years. It was used often and always in a mean-spirited, downright cruel manner. Never let them see me cry became my mantra.

Bit by bit, I became more self-conscious, and soon my parents despaired of me tearing up and throwing out every school picture. I became a mas-ter ripper; fastest fingers in the West (more accu-rately in Central Canada, but "the West" just rolls off the tongue better).

Braces resolved the problem eventually. They were fun. Steely bands wrapped around each tooth. Tracks of metal with little wires that would often break and cut my cheeks. Rubber bands popping out as I lisped my words. And the headgear. Dear God, the headgear. Orthodontists use Invisalign now. Kids today. I'll bet they don't walk miles uphill both ways to school anymore, either.

I'd like to say that I was able to slough off the negative early in life like Luna manages to do, but I hung on to those words and the feelings they generated for too freaking long. I think that it's the opposite of the beer-bellied former high school football star who carries that innate feeling of attractiveness with him as he strides through life. Speaking as one who didn't know her own self-worth for far too long, I wish that this magical confidence elixir could be bottled and sold. I'd have been first in line. (Unless someone else was in line behind me, in which case I would let them go first, of course.)

Darn those early years and their impact. I'm frustrated with myself though, for letting the words and opinions of others affect my self-esteem; I let the bastards grind me down.

Looking at the big picture, however, my elementary and high school years were positive, enough so that I chose to spend the rest of my life in the classroom. Things happen to everyone that affect self-esteem. Sometimes you just need to drop the baggage and keep moving. Steamer trunks are too darn heavy to keep lugging around, so I try to keep it to an overnight bag now. (Unless I get myself a bellman, in which case any unresolved emotional turmoil is welcome to rejoin my travels.) Opening up to someone you trust about pain/shame helps keep the luggage lighter. You realize that you're not alone and then its power is diminished.

Luna doesn't even need luggage. When her shoes get stolen, she happily goes barefoot.

Long live Luna.

✷ ✷ ✷

There is power in not caring what other people think. It usually stops a bully in his or her tracks. It can even stop a wannabe obscene caller.

My roommate was dating a fellow who worked nights at a pizza place and would often come by quite late. On the night in question, I had heard that he might be popping over. He was a guy with a good sense of humour who liked to joke around.

I fell asleep early that night but was awakened by the phone ringing beside my bed. I groggily answered it and heard a male voice say, "Do you know where my hand is?"

Assuming it was Boyfriend Bob calling the house line, I answered, "I hope it's on a big pizza."

Nothing.

Then, in a marginally frustrated tone I heard again, "I *said*, do you know where my hand is?"

I replied, "I'm going to go with: on a deep-dish with lots of olives, mushrooms, and sausage."

Silence.

Voice raised, "I *said*, DO YOU KNOW WHERE MY...oh, f*ck this!"

Slam.

Clearly not on a pizza. Perhaps the sausage wasn't far off, though.

Bob was sound asleep in the next room.

I'd like to think that my lack of fear or reaction to Handyman caused him to give up for the night, maybe even entirely. Not losing my cool or getting upset gave him zero power, which is sometimes the most effective strategy. Although my response was unintended, it worked.

I recommend that Handyman tries ringing Pizza Delight the next time he feels like putting something in his hand. I'm sure the two are irrevocably connected in his mind now.

He might even salivate.

★ ★ ★

The #MeToo Movement changed the world forever. Like every other social movement in life, sometimes the pendulum swings a little too far to one side to incite change before settling into the middle. It's a necessary swing, though, and I admire all women who have had the courage to call bullshit and push the pendulum. I look at our four kids and listen to how they talk about sexual consent and am filled with relief that they are growing up in a world where permission is needed, expected, and required.

When I get pregnant, my girls lead the way. Those suckers get huge. I mean it. I start bumping into things around me and spatial awareness goes right out the window. My seeing-eye pregnancy boobs help me navigate the world.

Eating dinner one evening with an elderly couple who were old family friends, I got up from the dining room table to get something in the tiny kitchen. The husband came in after me and my three-month-pregnant, clumsy breasts. I was picking up something from the counter when I turned around, and he was right there. He was so close that I leaned back into the counter with a nervous smile. What was happening? In seconds I felt both of his hands on my chest. He had a quick squeeze and fondle and then said with a wink, "Just checkin' to see if they're real."

He gave me his typical warm smile and then proceeded to turn around and get something from the fridge while I stood frozen against the counter. He chatted as if nothing had happened. To him, nothing had.

I had been violated by someone that I loved and trusted, someone who was like family. I was numb and in disbelief. Was it actually as bad as I thought?

I mean, come on Jackie, it was just a squeeze, after all. Maybe I was overreacting. Did I give some sign that I would be cool with that? These were the thoughts running through my brain. I've learned since that they're common thoughts in this situation. I can put it in context now as I imagine how I would feel if Molly or Madelynn were to go through this; it's funny how being outside of a situation can give you instant clarity.

I didn't say anything to either the husband or the wife about what had happened. Why not? Because I didn't want to cause problems or hurt anyone.

I went back to that dining room table and had my tea, smiling on the outside but sick to my stomach on the inside. I truly think that Handsy would have been shocked and devastated to know that I felt violated, which just goes to show you how deeply messed up and accepted the sexual culture was for so long.

I still loved him and grieved when he died. He'd been in my life for over twenty years. I try to remember all the good memories—and there were many. I never felt quite the same about him though, and continue to remain conflicted in my feelings. His roving hands stripped me of a sense of trust and safety that day, which is hard to forgive.

When I hear the younger generation use the word "consent," I feel gratitude. I can't say I ever talked about consent as a young, single, adult, nor did I hear anyone else talking about it either.

We've come a long way, and thank goodness for that.

✳ ✳ ✳

Getting back into the dating game as a newly divorced woman was daunting. I'm not even talking about the whole *oh my God, someone else is going to see me naked after all of these years; I'm going to need to get me a Weedwacker* thing.

No, merely dipping a toe into that whole world again was overwhelming. Online dating? At first, it felt like being a kid in a candy store. I could sit at my desk in my living room at my computer (before swiping was a thing), clicking through picture after picture of men. I could have had a face mask on and hair in curlers, and no one would have been the wiser. I could lounge from afar and pick out exactly what I was looking for with no more effort required than finger-clicking. Evident sense of humour? Gainfully employed? Doesn't write, "I seen?" Friendly eyes? Oh—and arms. I do like me some nice arms. Double-click.

This was fun.

Until it was not fun.

I went on two dates. Two.

The first was with a lovely man. He had an interesting job as a college professor, had invented an incredibly successful product, and built a beautiful house in the country off the grid. He was also outdoorsy. Like scaling mountains routinely before breakfast as a warm-up kind of outdoorsy.

This was not meant to be. My first hint was when my date asked to meet for a walk in a park in a neighbouring town. A walk sounded lovely to me. In the park. Filled with vibrant activity.

A walk. Ha.

It was a full-on hike. Isolated. Scaling wet rocks aside a waterfall. Off the beaten track.

I was prepared for all eventualities. I had read all the safety rules for online dating: Let friends know where you're going to be. Meet in a public venue. Stay around other people. He seemed lovely, though. And so excited. It was cute how excited he was.

Possibly being raped and murdered versus hurting his feelings—it was a toss-up.

The coin was in the air.

I broke it to him gently that it wasn't meant to be. Luckily he was a gentleman and took it well, and I moved on to my next date with renewed promises to be a safety girl.

Double-click number two led me to a widowed gentleman. He owned his own business in a beautiful town about an hour away. His eyes looked kindly, and he wrote romantically and movingly about life after loss. This had potential. We agreed to meet for a drink at a restaurant. In a public venue.

We ordered a drink and settled in with the slightly uncomfortable small talk that was the nature of the beast. Within minutes he pointed to a picture of a tower flashing across the mounted TV screen. He said, "What about that whole 9/11 thing? Conspiracy, right? American government was behind it all along."

I politely disagreed, and an uncomfortable silence ensued.

He then proceeded to flag down a waiter and order supper. This was supposed to be just a quick get-to-know-you drink. I tried to demur but was overruled as he quickly ordered for me too. Did I get up and leave? Oh no. Despite every last instinct in my body screaming to run for the hills as this horror show derailed further, I did not.

Instead, I tried to make the best of it. I expressed my condolences about the loss of his wife, to which he replied, "Hell no. That b*tch wasn't my wife. We just shacked up. She screwed around anyway, so I wasn't too broken up. The old lady before her screwed around on me too."

I'm a very slow eater, but I scarfed that

gluten-free spaghetti down as fast as I could and then beat a hasty retreat.

To my couch, a good book and a glass of wine.

Where I thought of a million and one things I could've/should've/would've said or done.

Thus ended my life as an online dater.

✳ ✳ ✳

Years ago, bathing on an island in Greece, I watched people of all shapes and sizes strut their stuff topless. One day, I promised myself I, too, would have the body confidence to do the same. The day has not yet arrived. I fear that I have missed the moment.

I'm not unsightly. People tend not to avert their gaze in horror as I pass by on the street. I'm not overly large either. There's no discreet kerfuffle with flight attendants trying to find seat belt extenders when I fly. And yet the words "bathing-suit season" spark unrivalled fear in my heart.

Measuring tapes and I share a complicated history. I spent my teen years inhaling calories by the thousand in a desperate bid to bulk up. My twenties were pretty much the body sweet spot and passed by sorely unappreciated. In my thirties, I teeter-tottered with weight throughout my pregnancies. And the last twenty years have been a Groundhog Day cycle of losing a few/gaining a few more pounds. God bless the inventor of the pull-on pant. My stuffed-to-the-brim wardrobe is proof that "fat" clothes and "skinny" clothes can live together in perfect harmony. Side by side.

Asking the nurse to take my blood pressure *before* having me step on the scale has become the norm at physicals. She patiently waits as I remove shoes, jewellry, belts, clothing, fake eyelashes, body hair—anything that might push along the ole arrow.

Overweight? BMI chart, you know nothing. Nothing, I say.

I fully support eating your feelings.

No one is hiding behind a sand dune, stealthily snapping my picture anymore as I exit the water tossing my damp mane. The thigh gap is a mere slit. Instead, I scour the internet each spring for suck-it-all-in bathing suits. Miracle suits don't actually work miracles, sadly. I vacillate between going all out on the old-lady look and buying the skirt-bottom or rocking the "board" shorts (for all the boarding I do, you know). Trying suits on in person at the shopping malls is no longer an option. I blame it all on the change room lighting. Fluorescent bulbs should be illegal.

Last August, I looked up momentarily from my own reflection in the water and observed the sun-dwellers cavorting around me. Lo and behold, stretch marks, cellulite, and stomach rolls were more the norm than not.

Could it be? Gasp. I was … normal?

No one was pointing fingers at me and chortling under their sunhats.

The bod's not likely to get any better going forward. Maybe it's time to take off my cover-up.

Baby steps.

✳ ✳ ✳

I had my hair done one day by a young, vibrant girl who was a pleasure to spend time with. She was the perfect mix of chatty/quiet for a hairdresser. After the initial catch-up and "What would you like done?" conversation was over, I settled in with the accessible, well-thumbed *People* and *Us* magazines, ready to catch up on the stars' shenanigans. Who had split up? Who was dating? Who was "just like me," and most importantly, who wore it best?

Exciting times.

Deep into the lives of the rich and famous, I didn't look up until it was all a done deal. And then suddenly – there I was: a vision. Perhaps not one of loveliness. Not golden blonde or strawberry blonde as requested.

White. White blonde. White blonde with my

pasty, pale complexion (and not of the English rose variety either).

What did I do?

Why, I smiled, Dear Readers. I smiled and thanked her profusely. Then I tipped. Generously.

And went home. And cried.

Lest you think I am exaggerating, the looks of horror on my students' faces as I walked into the room Monday morning would have convinced you.

The next day my lovely hairdresser showed up at the school. One of my students had gone home and, over the dinner table, recounted just how appalling I looked. Her mom was friends with another hairdresser who passed the story along at the salon.

Six degrees is real.

The poor stylist felt awful and offered to have me come in for free. She would fix my "do," she promised.

She tried. She failed. She didn't charge me, but I tipped her for her time anyway.

Generously.

I don't return bloody, rare steak when I ask for medium either.

I'm sensing a trend.

✳ ✳ ✳

The words "Border Crossing" strike fear in my heart. Those guards can be a wee bit intimidating. I mean, I suppose it is their job. Protect the country and all that.

The first time I crossed alone into the United States, en route to visit my siblings, I tried to be calm. Deep breaths, Jackie. The long lineup had given me plenty of time to prepare for all potential questions, my passport was in hand, and I rolled up to the window with relative confidence.

I offered up a cheery, "Hi there!" (first sign of a clear novice) with a little wave. He didn't wave back. "Take off your sunglasses" (second sign of a crossing fledgling). Why was I visiting? Where and with whom was I staying? Length of visit? Answers tripped off my tongue with relative ease. Any plants, fruit, or animals? Firearms? Drugs or alcohol? Zero.

Just as he was reaching out to return my passport, a thought crossed my mind, I broke out into a cold sweat, and my arm froze. I blurted out, "No, wait! *I do*! I *do* have alcohol! I have two coolers in the trunk! I *am* a smuggler!"

Two lonely little coolers, long since forgotten, nestled in the far corner of my white Impala.

He stared at me. Unblinking. And then, impassive,

with no expression in his voice uttered, "You. Party. Girl. What flavour?"

You can make friends anywhere, really.

It's good to be impervious to the opinions of others. But if you are going to care, border crossing guards should probably make your list.

LIFE LESSON #9

WHAT OTHER PEOPLE THINK OF YOU TRULY IS NONE OF YOUR BUSINESS.

Kamala Harris stated firmly, with a hand held up, "Mr. Vice President, I'm speaking" when interrupted. She didn't let the opinions of the millions of people watching sway her points, and she didn't let agreeableness stop her from being heard. That takes confidence.

Developing confidence over time is doable. Try new things, often hard and/or scary new things. Every successful experience helps pad your belief-in-yourself-resume.

I started a Glee Club years ago with zero background knowledge but a ton of faith. I decided, apropos of nothing one year, to plan and lead a whole-school flash mob. I wrote and directed school plays and led our staff in singing performances and dance-off competitions. I took dance classes. It's possible that I was kicking when I should have been turning, but I was in the moment. I took up singing which, although I'm not terribly skilled at it, brought me enormous joy.

I could have listened to negative comments or been derailed by the thought that these ventures might fail. I could have stayed in my comfort zone and avoided trying anything new, but I didn't.

When I chose the road less travelled by and took off on my own to live around the world, there were a lot of naysayers. In making that decision though, I not only gained life experience but a lot of trust and belief in myself as well. Sometimes you have to be a little bit deaf to other opinions and just follow your gut.

Confidence begets confidence.

A friend of mine was diagnosed with a tumour on her brain stem that most surgeons deemed inoperable. The fact that she survived the surgery and came out as she said, "still alive and still me" was a miracle. Spinal fluid leaks caused intensely painful complications, but she persevered through those with her trademark humour. She posted a picture of herself on Facebook, back to the camera, wearing an open hospital gown and the lovely (as all women who have given birth are familiar with) hospital diaper pad. She captioned the photo, "46, Diaper and Walker." That takes guts. Maybe almost dying puts not caring about what other people think into perspective.

I scored high on "Agreeableness" on that Big Five Personality Traits Test. It's nice to be nice.

I like to be liked. But when I have a strong opinion on something, I'm trying harder to express it these days and not care as much about how it will be received. You don't want to be a steamroller and belittle anyone who doesn't concur, but balance is a good thing.

Be polite but firm. Ruffle some feathers. Some things are worth it. I have miles to go.

A friend sent me her new mantra: "Why in the hell should I care what everybody else thinks? I don't even like everybody else."

Pink doesn't care. As she told her daughter, "Okay. So, Baby Girl. We don't change. We take the gravel and the shell and we make a pearl. And we help other people to change so they can see more kinds of beauty."

Pink is the best colour.

CHAPTER TEN

WHAT A RIDE

I took out the side mirror of an Audi once. It met with an unfortunate accident involving a garage-door frame. It wasn't my Audi; it belonged to the family that had hired me to be a live-in nanny. They were lovely people and it speaks volumes about their generous natures that they didn't deduct the mirror from my salary.

My husband gently tells me now that my unerring ability to "park by feel" perhaps isn't something to be proud of.

I like mirrors, though, especially in vehicles. They're rather handy. Have there been times when I may not have utilized them as much as I should have? C'est possible. Do I really need to look backwards?

My dad would have said "yes, actually."

The summer heat was starting to fade and a few lone leaves had turned colour early, heralding the beginning of fall. September in 1986 meant back to university for Jackie. Residence was a thing of the past and student housing was in the cards. Dad borrowed a pickup truck and The Dynamic Duo set off. Bed frames, side tables, cushions, desk, and mattresses got stuffed into that sturdy sucker. There must have been at least a few ropes around our precious cargo, but there's a chance that it remained unfettered; the details are a tad fuzzy.

Dad started off driving but, as is the often the deal when living with narcolepsy, tiredness hit and we switched places. He closed his eyes for a nap, I turned on the tunes, and we traversed happily down Highway 4. The sun was shining. Life was good.

Dad woke up on the outskirts of London and we pulled into the driveway of my new home. We got out of the truck at the same time, chatting cheerfully, and moseyed around to the back.

The cheerful chatting stopped. Eyes wide, we stared at the back of the truck. We stared at each other. We stared at the truck. The bed frame was there. So were the side tables, cushions, and desk.

The large, white, hard-to-miss double mattress, however, was glaringly absent.

I have visions of me, merrily careening down the highway, tapping my fingers on the steering wheel to the radio, while a lone white double mattress flies out the back. Family lore holds that several cars behind us were taken out by the mattress as it cartwheeled between lanes before smacking down on an innocent, minding-its-own-business wind-shield. According to my siblings (when drinks and memories evoke this story), the mattress flew from vehicle to vehicle, drivers were blinded, and a giant pileup ensued while Jackie blithely bopped along to Wham's "Wake Me Up Before You Go-Go."

We never found the mattress. I like to believe that it was put to good use.

At the time, I generously appointed Dad as an equal in the blame department. After all, the spotter in a boat is supposed to check to see if the water-skier falls. Shouldn't automobile wingmen be in charge of making sure furniture doesn't desecrate a highway? This excuse didn't fly with anyone, though, and the mattress legend was born.

Now, as parents on our third child's university housing move, we have a Suburban.

It's probably good for all who dare to share a highway with me that it's enclosed.

* * *

I don't like going around a racetrack, much to my husband's chagrin. I get seasick. I can't even play Mario Kart. Merely viewing a car race for more than a few minutes sparks waves of nausea. But watching camels race on a 10-kilometre oval track in the open desert outside of Al Ahmad, Kuwait, was doable. There were steel bleachers for the spectators, set to one side of a dusty track, just over a set of sand dunes. Sinewy racing camels, jockeys mounted atop, were assembled outside of a gate decorated with a large Kuwaiti flag. I believe now the camels have robotic jockeys, but at the time it was the real deal. Several teachers had gathered to watch the races that afternoon alongside men garbed in white dishdashas and women in black abayas. I was filled with excitement. As a horse-racing fan in my high school years, I was eager for the experience.

Camels are slower than racehorses in a sprint but can still run a good forty kilometres per hour. I watched the jostling camels and barefooted jockeys at the starting line as the race began and cheered alongside the small crowd as they galloped around the track. A cameraman and judges kept pace with the camels in a pickup truck.

After an afternoon spent cheering for camels

(belonging to parents from our school), my voice was hoarse. I was introduced to a few of the jockeys and animals and had an opportunity to admire them at close range. Just as I was casually patting and nodding along to general conversation (while nonchalantly dodging camel spittle) one of the men suggested that Miss Jackie try sitting on a winning camel for a photo op.

Climbing on the kneeling camel was easy. Trying to hang on while it straightened its tall, spindly back legs first, while still keeping its front legs down was more challenging. The blood rushed to my head until eventually all four of the camel's legs were firmly uncoiled beneath me. (I've ridden an elephant through the lush forests of Chiang Mai and I must say, elephants are far more comfortable and accommodating rides.) *Click* went the cameras as I proudly beamed and waved in my Toronto Blue Jays t-shirt.

Just then the owner slapped the rump of the camel and, with a "Yella, Miss Jackie" bellow and shout of raucous laughter, I was off.

Off.

Into the endless desert. Nothing but miles of sand in front of me.

I held on to my brazen hussy for dear life as the sounds of laughter behind me grew fainter. My racing heartbeat pulsated in my throat and my hands clenched tightly around the reins. It took a few seconds before I could clearly process what was happening and realized that the likelihood of me disappearing forever on a highly expensive camel (carrying a priceless Miss Jackie) was slim.

I let my breath out, relaxed my shoulders, and looked around. The sun was shining, golden dunes surrounded me, and I, well I was riding a freakin' camel across a freakin' desert.

For a moment the never-ending chatter in my mind ceased. Although I couldn't see a clear path ahead, that spicy camel knew exactly where it was going.

I just needed to hold on.

There really wasn't much I could do to change things. Maybe strength and wisdom would be needed shortly, but in the interim, serenity was the clear choice.

Eventually another rider caught up and led us back to the track. My former little minx of a camel now followed sedately along behind, suitably chastened.

And I … I closed my eyes and smiled.

✳ ✳ ✳

I'm directionally challenged. Thank God for the invention of the GPS. I can read a map when push comes to shove, and I know my left from my right, but that's about as good as it gets.

One fall day, after living in our new, cloistered, pandemic-riddled world for seven months, Dave and I decided to go on a road trip. Our destination was a beautiful little town about an hour and a half away. It overlooked a gorge and had lovely paths beside a river to stop and see the view at various lookout spots.

We listened to podcasts as we drove along, pausing to debate the latest *Armchair Expert* episode when so desired until we reached our destination. A perfect parking spot appeared, and we wandered over to the start of a trail that wound its way alongside the river. The sun was out, a light breeze rustled red, orange, and golden leaves, and all felt right with the world. It was as if we'd just exited a plane and landed on the tarmac of a foreign country after months of being clamped down in our little town. We walked, chatted, posed for pictures and enjoyed the view.

After a bit, we crossed a bridge and started back along the opposite side of the river. We were beginning to feel peckish, and, suffering from plantar fasciitis, my feet were starting to hurt.

Dave and I chatted some more—about everything and nothing. Until one of us (read: not me) finally realized that we should have been back about twenty minutes ago.

How could this be? We had followed the river down one side, crossed a bridge, and were following it back down the opposite side back to the town and our truck.

At this point, it would have been wise for us to stop and check our location on our phones. But no—we were old school (or just old) and felt like that would be simply ridiculous. There was literally no way we could have gotten off-course. The river was in plain sight to our left.

Until we noticed that there were campsites all around us. Empty campsites. Miles of them with little offshoots to circular lanes in every direction around a conservation area.

Using our stellar powers of deduction, we carefully absorbed all evidence: we were lost.

The river apparently branched off, and we had followed a cute little willowy branch of rushing water. Phones came out, and we discovered that it would be faster to forge our way ahead and circle around rather than backtrack.

Feeling as adventurous as teens at a gravel-pit party, we jumped barbed-wire fences (or rather climbed slowly with great trepidation) and crossed water-filled trenches. At long last we came to a road and began the long walk back to town, with me limping across the finish line when we finally reached the parking lot.

All totaled, we added an extra two and a half hours to our walk. Not a single cross word or exasperated sigh escaped our lips during that time. Once we figured out where we were and how to get back, we spent the minutes listening to music. We played our favourite songs for each other and answered online quizzes. We stopped and admired beautiful farmhouses and gorgeous properties along the way.

I have a picture of Dave standing in the middle of that seemingly endless road with his arms outstretched and a huge smile that perfectly encapsulates our trip.

The Day of the Lost Bearings.

A very happy day.

✶ ✶ ✶

I've learned that I do well in situations beyond my control. I'm a dab hand at relinquishing. I don't get stressed on airplane rides, for example. Once in the air, there really isn't anything I can do to change the outcome of a flight, so I just relax. Except for the time luggage flew all over the plane, a soccer team of students (all unencumbered by seat belts) flew out of their seats like rag dolls, and people started praying aloud. We made an emergency landing in

Qatar. I might not have been Thich Nhat Hanh to a T that time, but remained fairly calm, all things considered.

Hot-air ballooning one autumn day, a friend in the group nervously questioned the operator when told we were going higher than we were currently floating. When the operator responded serenely with, "Doesn't make much difference if we crash from this height or higher. The end result would be the same," I felt … peace. Things were beyond my control, and I went with the moment.

When I have the power to make a difference with my actions and choices, things get trickier for me. I'm not much of an alpha. Not really a beta either. I don't know how far down the alphabet you would have to go to nail my status but suffice it to say, it might be a ways.

I looked forward to a full day of dog sledding with anticipation. Dogs were great— loved 'em. Snow, peace, woods, fields—check, check, check, check. Lunch cooked over a campfire and eaten outdoors while sitting on logs—I could live with that. Peeing in the great outdoors while wearing a snowsuit—the jury was out.

Driving down the long, winding laneway leading to the dog sledding company, the sight of the wood-beamed home surrounded by forests me reciting Robert Frost in my head. The owners introduced my fellow visitors and me to their gorgeous Alaskan Malamutes. Becoming a dog musher was not a spectator sport, we were told. Lessons were given, including learning the proper handling and operation of the sled and equipment. Standing on the runners, holding onto the handlebar, the brake in the centre was demonstrated. It was used for speed and steering, with importance placed on keeping the harness line tense, so the dogs didn't get tangled up. Balancing our weight left or right helped with the steering. The owners demonstrated how to harness and hook up the team and had the guests try. Two people would go with each team of six dogs, taking turns as driver and dog handler. We learned the new language quickly: *Hike!* got the dogs moving. *Gee!* (right) *Haw!* (left), *Easy!* (slow down) and *Whoa!* (stop). My ability to pick up tricky new lingo is noteworthy—I'm basically a polyglot.

The dogs were chosen and attached to the line. Leaping and twisting, a cacophony of howls filled the air; these beauties were ready to rock and roll. Every fibre of their being screamed, *let us pull*.

We were off. As we raced along, the sleigh runners gliding over the snowy surface, the frenzied barks abated, and soon we were surrounded by the sound of silence. The snow absorbed the sound of the sleigh as we raced away from the havoc of daily life.

We had had a storm overnight, and it was tough going for our furry friends, which translated into tough going for their novice mushers. Jumping off the sled and running along through the deep, fresh snow, especially up hills, became more and more necessary as the day wore on. Soon, despite the cold temperature, sweat dripped down our faces. If you ever want a good cardio workout, go dog-sledding. No leotard is required.

Pristine snow carpeted the ground and covered the surrounding trees as the sun shone in the sky overhead. Standing on the runners, flying around corners and racing down slopes, my beaming smile said it all. I wasn't worried about bill payments, my to-do list, work, my kids, my hair (fine, thin, and perpetually frizzy)—anything at all, really. My focus was on gliding, running, steering, braking – there wasn't room for anything other than being in the moment.

The trail was indiscernible to our novice eyes but easily followed by the dogs. I wish that in my real world I had someone telling me *Gee!* or *Haw!* with certitude when I reached a fork in my road. Life would be a whole lot easier. I'm well-versed in second-guessing myself, so being told it was time to *Whoa!* or *Hike!* would definitely come in handy too. Learning to drive my own sled in life, especially when trudging was required, was a skill that needed refining.

A little trust in myself and my team, persever-ance, being the lead dog when necessary, taking time out to embrace the moment—I learned a lot that snowy day.

✳ ✳ ✳

It's been a long and winding road, but I can finally, finally say with confidence that I am hot.

Smokin' hot, in fact.

Oh yes, I am.

And then I'm cold.

And then I'm hot again.

And my face is puce and rivulets of perspiration trickle down my body. And I surreptitiously wipe sweat stains off of friends' chairs—pretending to pick up some nondescript item that has purport-edly fallen by the wayside. And I lie in bed all hours of the night trying to remember the myriad things I have forgotten in my fog-like existence. My hus-band quickly learned to gauge the depths of my moodiness from afar.

A veritable red-faced, slick, butter-fingered, sleep-deprived, easily vexed goddess.

I used to dread menopause. The thought of the possibility—if not improbability—of giving birth to an Audrey or Tom ripped from my useless uterus rendered me forlorn. Briefly. Until my periods became so horrifically *Carrie*-esque and painful that I welcomed the dawn of the age of the barren with open arms.

I'd like to go gracefully into that good night. Or at least that evening. But, alas, little about this forty-three year journey has been graceful. From getting my first period while sitting in my grade seven class, to years of labour-like monthly pain, to finding clothes big enough to drape over my bloated belly, to the hell of the dreaded hot flashes—it has all been quite a ride.

Ride or die, Baby. Not many other options along the feminine road.

I hold onto the hope, however, that the end of this road is in sight. I've said au revoir to hypothetical Audrey and Tom in my head and am ready to be a kick-ass grandma instead.

I support young pregnancy.

But the terrain has not quite been covered yet. To add insult to injury, I currently have a foot in two lands. Buying tampons while asking the clerk at the pharmacy for the senior's discount surely must warrant my acceptance into an elite group of women.

I've always coveted the thought of my name being added to *The World Book of Records*; this could be my chance.

I know that there are options. I've read Suzanne Somers' books. But I have a lifelong aversion to medication that keeps me deeply entrenched in the "complaining about it" camp rather than the "take action" clique.

In my defense, aversion has been steeped in family tradition. My grandmother has never met a medication with which she's become more than casually acquainted. She soldiered on through the peri- and menopausal years with nary a drug. Perhaps we're masochists by nature. But hey, the woman is going to hit a hundred, so I'm all for following the leader.

Apparently, there are pros and cons of being a late-to-the-party menopausal woman. Current research purports that I've got a lower risk of clutching my chest as I fall to the ground, will live longer than the average bear, and will remember where I left my glasses. Conversely, I'd better pencil in some time to have my breasts crushed between mammoth, icy metal bookends. Staring at the ceiling, opening my legs and thinking of England while a spatula scrapes away at my cells for a few more years is also on the books.

Nothing comes for free.

I like to think of myself as generous. A fill-a-bucket, pay-it-forward, spread-kindness-like-confetti kind of girl. Perhaps not in the blanket-sharing department, however, especially during menopause. Months of flipping and flopping on our queen-sized bed, covers on, covers off, covers yanked and covers tossed, eventually drove even my mild-mannered husband to distraction.

Cue the purchase of The Split-King Bed. No matter how often my husband dubs it The Divorce Bed, he's the first to admit that it has saved our sanity. While a concerted effort is required to cross the great divide, he is now able to sleep right through the dreaded night sweats.

At least he can honestly brag to his buddies that his wife is a smokeshow.

This too shall pass.

But maybe that's not as good as I think it will be.

I have spent so many minutes, hours, weeks, and months of my life wishing time away. I need to remember that all the twists, turns, and pit stops of the journey represent actual years of my actual life.

I spent my teens racing along Officially a Woman Now Street. Then detoured through my twenties down the side-road, Please Don't Let Me Be Pregnant Avenue. Which was followed by a few spins around I'm Ready to Bear Children Court in my thirties. And then cruised along Please, For The Love of Everything Holy, Have Some Snippage Done Lane. I'm currently merging slowly onto Route Oh My God, I'm Barren, puttering towards my final destination, My Bones Are As Brittle As Uncooked Pasta, My Wrinkly, Prune-like Face Scares The Crap Out Of Me, And I'd Give Anything For A Shot Of Estrogen To Get Me Through 'Til Lunchtime Parking Lot.

ETA to be determined.

Still I complain. I've moaned and bellyached every step of the way along the path. Maybe it's time to make the most of the view – even if I don't always love what I see.

Although I can still get a good bang for my buck with a winning *Cash for Life* ticket, I'm starting to run out of rerouting options.

LIFE LESSON #10

KEEP YOUR EYES ON THE ROAD AND BE PRESENT.

Everyone has stories. It just takes looking in the rearview mirror to find them. Looking backwards can help you make sense of your life, remind you how far you've come, and help you gain empathy for yourself. Looking forward is good, too. It gives you something to be excited about and keeps you feeling optimistic and motivated. But keeping your gaze directly on the road in front of you (while briefly glancing back and ahead) is probably the best of all.

It keeps you present.

Taking accountability for where you are on the road as you drive is vital (and something I continue to work on). Without accountability you're just going to keep finding yourself traversing the same damned stretch of highway ad infinitum.

Looking back over my life has helped me to realize how far I've come and how far I still want to go. I'm a work in progress. I still get defensive on days that end in "ay," care too much about other peoples' opinions, and judge more than I'd like.

But for the most part, I'm happy with where I am. Andy Bernard from *The Office* confided that he wished there was a way of knowing you were in the good old days while you're actually in them. I guess that's the whole "living in the moment" bit.

I read a storybook to my classes that I love called *Miss Rumphius*, based on the true story of a woman's life. Her goal was to do three things: travel to far-off places, live by the water, and make the world a more beautiful place. I think that's a pretty good road map. I've done well on the travel bit, and I live in a truly gorgeous town on the shores of Lake Huron. Make the world a more beautiful place? I'm not sure about this one, but I hope that I've made it a little kinder and happier for some children along the way—especially my own. Miss Rumphius planted lupines all over her small town. I have fake plants hanging outside of my house. I'll keep working on her last goal.

Maybe I'll scatter a few seeds as I drive along my road.

There's no pace car.

EPILOGUE

And so …

When the day comes that you find yourself lying flat on your back on a damp bathroom floor, covered in thick globs of green paint, being asked to help with someone else's bowel movement, know that you're not alone.

Clean yourself off, arise and go to Innisfree … and … be happy. Green-paint moments are just a part of life; we might as well make the most of them.

Looking back over my own stories helps me to be a little bit more tolerant and understanding of people around me. It also allows me to relate more readily to others; laughter is a great connector. We're all just fumbling our way through life.

Life isn't always funny. Climate change, global

pandemics, school shootings, reversal of rights, war, even murder hornets ... it often feels like we're bombarded with horrific news at every turn. Sometimes it's hard to find things to laugh about. Through all the ups and downs though, I try to find something to smile at—even if, often, it's just me. Humour doesn't negate the painful moments, but it sure does make them more bearable.

Look back on your life and learn. Look forward in life and dream. Enjoy the moment and notice. Be unequivocally and unapologetically yourself. But most of all, laugh.

We only get one kick of the can at this thing called life. Kick it with a smile.

ACKNOWLEDGEMENTS

I would like to start with a shout-out to my uncle, Bruce Ewing. His wonderful books chronicling the Ewing family history inspired me to put pen to paper. My dad, Curt Ewing, also influenced me with his version of *Life Lessons*. Braeden Griffiths' vulnerability and honesty in his own creative endeavours inspired me to be brave.

My early readers, Deb Walpole, Anita Boyce, Sandra Matthews, Karla Uliana, and Nancy Gray-Starkebaum, along with my family, gave me invaluable feedback, support, and encouragement. Thanks so much.

A huge thank you to Stephen Parolini and Kate Victory Hannisian for their insightful wisdom and expertise while editing and proofreading my work. Their patience and guidance with my newbie questions throughout this process are much appreciated. Some bits and pieces have been added since editing. Any mistakes are my own. Thanks also to the highly talented Jennifer Stimson for her creative and beautiful cover design and formatting. She captured the feel of my book perfectly. Kate Garland also deserves a big thank you for her talent and patience as my author- photographer. Much gratitude to all who let me publicly share our adventures–especially Mike Noel. I really do appreciate it.

While writing this book, I realized the very best life lesson of all: keep close to your friends and family as you age. They make the happy times infinitely more fun and the tough times better.

Many dear friends surfaced in this memoir (in the order in which I met them): Kim McClement, Susan Cobean, Paul Bolton, Lynn Worsley, Nancy Gray-Starkebaum, Sandra Matthews, Karla Uliana, Tessa Lamb, and Anita Smith-Kelly ... thank you. Several other close friends and family members did not make a guest appearance in *Life Lessons* but have also made my life decidedly more entertaining and rewarding.

Thank you. I treasure you all.

To my outlaws: Karen Morton and Richard Garland–you will always be inlaws to me–no point in fighting it. You are both Ewings-by-proxy.

Lisa Garland, Doug Ewing, and Dave Ewing – thank you. To quote the end of my grade seven speech: "Being one of four's more fun than being just the only one." I'm so lucky to be one of four with all of you.

A very special thank you to my mom and my dad – Lynne and Curt Ewing – who raised me to love books. I'm forever grateful to be their daughter.

Madelynn and Braeden Griffiths – thank you both. I love being your step-mom and am so proud of the cool adults you've become. I'm currently hard at work on our next scavenger hunt. (I know you're breathless with anticipation.)

Molly and Finn Noel – you make everything worthwhile. My greatest joy is being your mom. I learn from you both daily.

Finally, my deep gratitude and love to my husband, Dave Griffiths. My first and last reader, my confidant, rock, daredevil, and biggest fan. You were worth the wait.

***

If you would like to contact Jackie Ewing you can email her at: **jackieauthorewing@gmail.com**

Manufactured by Amazon.ca
Bolton, ON